Thomas Perkins

Wimborne Minster and Christchurch Priory

A Short History of Their Foundation and Description of Their Buildings

Thomas Perkins

Wimborne Minster and Christchurch Priory
A Short History of Their Foundation and Description of Their Buildings

ISBN/EAN: 9783337003012

Printed in Europe, USA, Canada, Australia, Japan

Cover: Foto ©ninafisch / pixelio.de

More available books at **www.hansebooks.com**

WIMBORNE MINSTER

AND

CHRISTCHURCH PRIORY

A SHORT HISTORY OF THEIR FOUNDATION AND DESCRIPTION OF THEIR BUILDINGS

BY THE

REV. THOMAS PERKINS

M.A., F.R.A.S.

RECTOR OF TURNWORTH, DORSET

WITH ILLUSTRATIONS FROM
PHOTOGRAPHS BY THE
AUTHOR

LONDON GEORGE BELL & SONS 1899

AUTHOR'S PREFACE

WHEN writing the chapters of the present volume which treat of Wimborne Minster, the author consulted the last edition of Hutchins' "History of Dorset," which contains a considerable amount of somewhat ill-arranged information on the subject, verifying all the descriptions by actual examination of the building; similarly, when preparing the part of this volume dealing with Christchurch Priory, he made some use of "The Memorials of Christchurch Twynham," written originally by the Rev. Mackenzie Walcott, F.S.A., and revised after his death in 1880 by Mr B. Edmund Ferrey, F.S.A. He also consulted papers on the subject that have appeared from time to time in various periodicals and MSS. that were kindly placed at his disposal by the Secretary of the Society for the Protection of Ancient Buildings.

He desires to express his thanks to the Vicars of the two churches for permission to thoroughly examine every part of the buildings, and to photograph them without let or hindrance; he also wishes to bear testimony to the readiness shown by the clerks and vergers in imparting local information and in facilitating his photographic work.

T. P.

October 1899.

CONTENTS

WIMBORNE MINSTER

PAGE

CHAPTER I.—History of the Building 3
  Date of Foundation 5
  The Norman Church 8, 9
  Alterations in the Thirteenth and Fourteenth Centuries . . 10, 11
  Alterations in the Fifteenth and Sixteenth Centuries . . 11, 12
  Modern Restorations 14

CHAPTER II.—The Exterior 16
  The Central Tower 16
  The North Porch 22
  The East Window 24
  The Sundial 25
  The South Porch 25
  The Western Tower 26

CHAPTER III.—The Interior 29
  The North Porch 29
  The Aisles 29, 38
  The Clerestory 33
  The Central Tower 34
  The Transepts 38
  The East End, Choir and Presbytery 42
  Sedilia and Piscina 44
  The Beaufort and Courtenay Tombs and Brass of Aethelred . 42, 47
  The South Choir Aisle and Etricke Tomb . . . 48
  The North Choir Aisle and Uvedale Monument . . 50, 51
  The Crypt, Vestry, and Library 52
  Deans of Wimborne 59

CHAPTER IV.—St Margaret's Hospital 60
  Dimensions of Wimborne Minster 63

CHRISTCHURCH PRIORY

CHAPTER I.—History of the Building 67
  Foundation 68
  The Norman Church 70
  Alterations in the Thirteenth—Fifteenth Centuries . . 71
  Modern Alterations 72

v

	PAGE
CHAPTER II.—The Exterior	76
The Western Tower	76
The North Porch	80
The North Aisle	80
The North Transept	82
The Choir, Presbytery, and Lady Chapel	84
The South Transept	88
The Nave	88
The Porter's Lodge, and Sites of the Domestic Buildings	89
CHAPTER III.—The Interior	92
The Nave	92-98
The Aisles	98
The Transepts	100
The Rood Screen	105
The Choir	106
The Choir Stalls	108-110
The Reredos	112
The Salisbury Chantry	116
The Draper Chantry	118
The Lady Chapel, and the " Miraculous Beam "	120
St Michael's Loft	126
The Shelley Monument	126
CHAPTER IV.—Deans, Priors, and Vicars of Christchurch	128
Stratford's Injunctions	129
Archbishop Arundel's Injunctions	130
The Norman Castle	131
The Norman House	132
Dimensions of Christchurch Priory	134

LIST OF ILLUSTRATIONS

WIMBORNE MINSTER

	PAGE
Arms of Wimborne and Christchurch	*Title page*
Wimborne Minster from the North-East	2
Wimborne Minster in 1840	3
Wimborne Minster in 1707. (From a copperplate in the Library) .	13
The Minster from the South-East before 1891	19
The North Transept before 1891	21
The East Window	23
The Western Tower	27
The Interior, looking East	30
Pier and Arch-Spring, South Arcade	31
Decorated Arch in the Nave	32
Clerestory Stage of the Central Tower	35
The Tower Arches	36
North Transept and Crossing	37
Thirteenth-Century Piscina, South Transept	39
Choir Stalls	40
West View from the Choir	41
The East Window	43
Sedilia	44
The Beaufort Tomb	45
Brass of Aethelred	46
The Etricke Tomb	49
Relic Chest	50
The Uvedale Monument	51
Entrance to Crypt	53
The Library	54
The Crypt	55
The Font	56
The Clock in the West Tower	57
St Margaret's Hospital	61

CHRISTCHURCH PRIORY

Christchurch Priory from the Bridge . . .	66
Christchurch Priory from the North-East . .	77
Tower Door	78
The North Porch . . . . ., . .	79

vii

PAGE

The North Door 81
The North Transept in 1810 83
The North Transept 85
South Aisle of Nave 87
The Nave in 1834 93
The Nave 95
North Arcade of the Nave 96
From the North Triforium 97
Bay of the Triforium, South Side 98
South Aisle of the Nave 99
The Montacute Chantry 101
North Aisle of the Nave 103
The Crypt 105
The Rood Screen 107
Stall Seats (3) 108
Choir Stalls 109
Miserere on Stall Seat (circa 1300) 110
The Choir 111
The Reredos 113
The Salisbury Chantry 115
Interior of the Salisbury Chantry 117
The Draper Chantry 119
Piscina in the Draper Chantry 120
The Sacristy 121
The Miraculous Beam 122
Tomb of Thomas, Lord West 123
The Lady Chapel 124
St Michael's Loft 125
Remains of the Norman House 133

Plans 136, 137

A

WIMBORNE MINSTER FROM THE NORTH-EAST.

WIMBORNE MINSTER

CHAPTER I

HISTORY OF THE BUILDING

OF the churches connected with the religious houses which once existed in the county of Dorset, three only remain to the present day. Of some of the rest we have ruins, others have entirely disappeared. But the town of Sherborne, once the bishop-stool of the sainted Aldhelm, who overlooked a vast diocese comprising a great portion of the West Saxon kingdom, has its Abbey now used as its Parish Church. The great Abbey of Milton, founded by Æthelstan, has handed down to us its choir and transepts—rebuilt in the fourteenth century, after the former church had been destroyed by fire—and this, though private property, is still used for occasional services ; and the minster church at Wimborne has became the church of the parish of Wimborne Minster.

The town has been by many supposed to stand on the site of the Roman Vindogladia, though this station has by others been identified with Gussage Cowdown, or the circular encampment of Badbury Rings, about three miles to the north-west of Wimborne Minster. Be this as it may, the district was

3

occupied by the Roman conquerors of our island; and
Roman pottery and other remains have been found in the
neighbourhood, including a small portion of pavement beneath
the floor of the minster church.

The derivation of the name Wimborne, or Winborne as we
find it sometimes written, has been much disputed; but as
we find the same word appearing as the name of several other
places which lie on the course of the same stream, now
generally called the Allen, though sometimes the Wim, it is
highly probable that the name is derived from that of the
river. Compound names for villages are very common in
Dorset—the first word being the name of the river on which
the village stands, the second being added to distinguish one
village from another. Thus we find along the Tarrant,
villages known as Tarrant Gunville, Tarrant Hinton, Tarrant
Launceston, Tarrant Monkton, etc.; and along the Winterborne
we find Winterborne Houghton, Winterborne Stickland,
Winterborne Clenstone, etc.; and in like manner we meet
with Monkton up Wimborne, Wimborne Saint Giles, and
Wimborne Minster along the course of the Allen. The
characteristic name of Winterborne for a brook that is such in
winter only, but is a dried-up bed in a hot summer is borne
by two streams in Dorset, each giving its name to a string of
villages. May not the word Wimborne or Winborne be a
contraction for this same word Winterborne, the "burn" of
the rainy winter months, applied to the little stream of the
Allen?

The small town of Wimborne Minster stands not far from
the junction of the Allen with the slow-running Dorset Stour,
in the midst of pleasant fertile meadow-land, from which
here and there some low hills rise. Its chief glory has been,
and probably always will be, its splendid church, with its central
Norman and its Western Perpendicular towers, its Norman
and Decorated nave, its Early English choir, and its numerous
tombs and monuments of those whose names are recorded in
the history of the country.

The exact year of the foundation of the original religious
house is differently given in various ancient documents: the
dates vary from 705 A.D. to 723 A.D. At this time, Ine was
king of the West Saxons; and one of his sisters, Cudburh—or
Cuthberga, as her name appears in its Latinised form—was

espoused or married to Egfred, or, as he is often called, Osric, the Northumbrian king, but the marriage was never consummated, and the lady as soon as possible separated from him and retired to the convent at Barking, and afterwards founded the convent at Wimborne. Some say that she objected to the intemperate habits of her espoused as soon as she met him; others, that having previously vowed herself to heaven, she persuaded him to release her from the engagement to him, which had been arranged without her wishes being consulted. Her sister Quinberga is stated to have been associated with her in the foundation of the religious house, and both were buried within its precincts, and both were afterwards canonised; Saint Cuthberga was commemerated on August 31st "as a virgin but not a martyr." A special service appointed for the day is to be found in a Missal kept in the Library of the Cathedral Church at Salisbury, in which the following prayer occurs:—

"Deus qui eximie castitatis privilegio famulam tuam Cuthbergam multipliciter decorasti, da nobis famulis tuis ejus promerente intercessione utriusque vitae prosperitatem. Ut sicut ejus festivitas nobiscum agitur in terris, ita per ejus interventum nostri memoria apud te semper habeatur in coelis, per Dominum etc."

There is reason to believe that the earliest date given above for the foundation (705 A.D.) is the most probable one, as Regner in his tracts mentions a letter bearing this date written by Saint Aldhelm, and taken from the register of Malmesbury, in which he includes in a list of congregations to which he grants liberty of election the monastery at Wimborne, presided over by the sister of the king. There is also some evidence for the existence of a community of monks at Wimborne, as well as of nuns. But of these original religious houses not a trace remains: the very position of St Cuthberga's Church is uncertain; we cannot be sure that the present building occupies the same site; the last resting-places of the two royal foundresses are not even pointed out by tradition. Probably the buildings were destroyed, the nuns slain or driven out, when the raiding Danes overran Wessex in the ninth century.

The next historical event that we meet with in connection with Wimborne is the burial of King Æthelred, the brother and immediate predecessor on the throne of the great West

Saxon king Ælfred. As there is doubt about the year of
the foundation by Cuthberga, so again there is a conflict of
testimony as to the date, place, and manner of the death of
Æthelred—the inscription on the brass (about which more
will be said when we come to describe the interior of the
minster) not agreeing with the usually accepted date for the
accession of Ælfred, 871; but as the brass is itself many
centuries later than the burial of the king whose likeness
it professes to bear, its authority may well be questioned.
Anyhow, Æthelred died either of wounds received in some
battle with the Danes, in some spot which different archæologists have placed in Surrey, Oxford, Berkshire, or Wilts, or
worn out by his long and arduous exertions while struggling
with the heathen invaders; and his body—this alone is
certain—was brought to Wimborne for burial. It has been
conjectured that Ælfred, after he had defeated the Danes and
established himself firmly on the throne of Wessex, would
naturally rebuild the ruined abbey. He founded, as we know,
an abbey at Shaftesbury; he is recorded to have built at
Winchester and London; he had undoubtedly a taste for
architecture, and he was a devout son of Mother Church, so
that it is by no means improbable that he would erect a
church over the grave of his brother: but no record of such
building remains, and there is no trace of any pre-Norman
work in the existing minster.

The original church and conventual buildings having been
swept away by the Danes, whether Ælfred restored it or not is
uncertain, but it is certain that a house of secular canons was
established at Wimborne by a king of the name of Eadward;
but again there is some uncertainty as to whether this king
was the one who is sometimes called the Eadward the Elder,
sometimes Eadward the Unconquered, son and successor of
Ælfred, or Eadward the Confessor. Anyhow, it became a
collegiate church and a royal free chapel, and as such it is
mentioned in Domesday Book, and it is noticed as a Deanery
in the charters of Henry III. Leland, writing in the reign of
Henry VIII., says, "It is but of late time that a dean and
prebendaries were inducted into it." The deanery was in the
gift of the Crown, and we have a full list of the deans from
1224 up to 1547, when it was dissolved. The ecclesiastical
establishment consisted of a dean, four prebendaries, three

vicars, four deacons, and five singing men.   It will not be needful to give any detailed account of these, as most of them, though in many cases they held other more dignified posts,* either together with the deanery or after resigning it, are not men who have made their mark in English history. A few only will here be mentioned, who on account of some circumstances connected with the fabric, or for other reasons, are more noteworthy.

Thomas de Bembre, 1350-1361, founded a chantry and an altar in the north part of the north transept, which was added at this time.

Reginald Pole, so well known in the history of the reigns of Henry VIII. and Queen Mary, was Dean of Wimborne from 1517 till 1537.   It is remarkable that he was only seventeen years of age at the time of his appointment.

He was succeeded by **Nicholas Wilson**, who held the office of dean until the dissolution of the deanery in 1547.   To him a curious letter still existing was addressed in 1538 by certain leading men of the parish, though nothing appears to have been done in consequence of it.   These worthy men complain of the dilapidated state of the church, the want of funds to carry out needed repairs, and suggest the taking from the church "seynt Cuthborow's hed," and "the sylv' y' ys about the same hed," which they claim as belonging to the parish on the ground that it was made by the charity of the parishioners in times past.   "Our chyrche," they say, "ys in gret ruyn and decay and our toure ys foundered and lyke to fall and ther ys no money left in õ chyrche box and by reason of great infyrmyty and deth ther hath byn thys yere in oure parysh no chyrche aele, the whych hath hyndred õ chyrch of xx^ti nobles and above, and well it is knowen y' we have no land but onely the charity of good people, wherfor nyed constraynyth us to sell the sylv' y' is about the same hed. Besechynge yo' mastership to sertefy us by y' tre wher we may sell the said sylv' to repayr õ chyrche."†

* It is noteworthy that they all held some other preferment during the time that they held the office of dean.

† In an inventory made in the reign of Henry VIII. we find mentioned an image of St Cuthberga, with a ring of gold, and two little crosses of gold, with a book and staff in her hand.   The head of the image of silver with a crown on it of silver and gilt.   On her apron a St James shell with a buckle of silver and gilt.

The names of many of the other ecclesiastics connected with the church are known: among these, we need only mention William Lorynge canon, who in the time of Richard II. caused the great bell called the Cuthborow bell to be made; and Simon Beneson, sacrist, who left land, which is called Bell Acre, towards the maintenance and repair of the bells.

Among other benefactors of the church was Margaret, Countess of Richmond, mother of Henry VII., so well known at Cambridge under the name of Lady Margaret, the foundress of Christ's and St John's Colleges. She founded at Wimborne the original seminary connected with the minster, which afterwards became by a charter of Elizabeth the Grammar School of the town, and presented splendid vestments to the church. July 9th was until the Reformation kept at the minster as a festival to her memory, with a special office and High Mass.

When the deanery was abolished, Wimborne Minster became a Royal Peculiar, under the administration of three priest-vicars elected by the Corporation. These served each for a month in turn. The Corporation had the power of appointing one of the three vicars—who was known as the "Official"—to hold courts and grant licences. The court was held in the western part of the north aisle, the Official presiding, seated at a desk, the two other vicars sitting one on each side of him, while at a long table sat the churchwardens, sidesmen, the vestry clerks, and the apparitors.

The arrangement by which the vicars served the church each in turn continued in force until 1876. At that time one of the three vicars retired on a pension; another removed to the chapelry of Holt, three miles from Wimborne (which had previously been served in turn by the vicars of Wimborne), a parsonage having been built for his accommodation; and the third became sole vicar of the minster church and the parish attached to it.

For the history of the fabric we have to trust almost entirely to the architectural features of the church itself, as documentary evidence is unusually scanty.

Nothing of earlier date than the twelfth century can be seen in Wimborne Minster, but we know pretty accurately, the extent and form of the Norman Church; for, during the course

of restoration undertaken in the present century, the foundations of some parts of this church were discovered beneath
the floor of the existing building, and other pieces of Norman
work formerly concealed, and now again concealed beneath
plaster, were laid bare. There is one interesting feature about
the church worthy of notice—namely, that the builders who
succeeded one another at the various periods of its history
did not, as a rule, destroy the work of their predecessors to
such an extent as we frequently find to have been the case
with the builders of other churches : possibly this may have
been due to the fact that at no time was Wimborne Minster
a rich foundation. There was no saintly shrine, there were
no wonder-working relics to attract pilgrims and gather the
offerings of the faithful and enrich the church in the way in
which the shrine of Saint Cuthbert enriched Durham, that of
the murdered archbishop enriched Canterbury, and that of
the murdered king enriched Gloucester. But, whatever the
reason may have been, we can but be thankful that the
mediæval builders destroyed so little at Wimborne ; while we
regret that modern restorers have not been as scrupulous in
preserving the work which they found existing, but have in
some instances endeavoured to put the church back again into
the state in which they imagined the fourteenth-century builders
left it.

We may regard the arches and lower stages of the central
tower as the oldest part now remaining in its original condition.
No doubt the Norman choir was the first to be built, as we
find that it was almost the universal custom to begin churches
at the eastern end, and gradually to extend the building
westward, as funds and time allowed. Here, however, as
in many other cases, the small Norman choir eastward of the
central tower in course of time was considered too small,
and the eastern termination had to be demolished to admit
of the desired extension to the east. Norman choirs, as a
rule, had an apsidal termination to the east, and it was
not till Early English times that square east ends, which were
characteristic of the English church in pre-Norman times,
prevailed again over the Norman custom ; and it is worthy of
notice that this rectangular termination towards the east end
remains a marked characteristic of the thirteenth-century
work in England, Continental church-builders having retained

the apsidal termination till the Renaissance.   The side walls
of the Norman choir extended two bays to the east of the
central tower, and the nave four bays westward of the same.
The transepts were shorter than at present, and the side
aisles of the nave narrower.   There appear to have been two
side chapels to the choir, extending as far as the first bay
eastward; beyond this to the east were two Norman windows
on each side: these windows, parts of which remain, cut off
by the Early English arches, were round-headed, and richly
ornamented with chevron mouldings.   They were uncovered
at the time of the restoration, but are now again hidden by
plaster.   At the south end of the south transept a low building seems to have existed: the walls of this were raised when
the south transept was lengthened in the fourteenth century.
The Norman masonry may be seen under the south window
of the transept, and a Norman string course runs round the
sides and ends of the present transept.   The aisles of the
nave were not only narrower, but were also lower, than those
now existing.   It is also probable that these aisles did not
originally extend as far westward as the nave.   The windows
of the Norman clerestory, which may still be seen from the
interior, though all similar in design, are not alike in workmanship.   The one over the narrow eastern bay on either
side differs from those over the three bays farther to the west.
Moreover, a continuous foundation has been discovered under-
neath the three western arches of the Norman nave.   Possibly
there was at one time a solid wall in this position, intended,
however, from the first only to be temporary, and this was removed when the aisles, still in Norman times, were lengthened.
The tower itself was not all built at the same time; the upper
stages are ornamented with an arcading of intersecting arches
indicating a somewhat later date.

In the thirteenth century the east end of the choir seems
to have been removed and the presbytery added: its date is
pretty clearly determined by the east window, in which we
notice some signs of the approaching change from the Early
English simple lancet into the plate tracery of the Decorated
period.   Rickman gives its approximate date as 1220.   During
the fourteenth century the nave aisles were widened and
extended farther west, and at the same time two bays were
added to the nave itself.   The Norman chapels on either

side of the choir were lengthened into aisles, not, however, extending as far to the east as the thirteenth-century presbytery; arches were cut in the Norman choir walls to give access to these new aisles. The transepts were lengthened, the south one by raising the walls of the Norman chapel mentioned above, which, it has been conjectured, was used as the Lady Chapel, the north transept by the addition of Bembre's chantry.

During the fifteenth century the western tower was built 1448—1464, and probably at the same time the walls of the nave were raised; and the roofs of the nave aisles, which had been much lower than now, so as not to block up the Norman clerestory windows, were raised on the sides joining the nave walls above the heads of these windows, and a new clerestory was formed in the raised wall. This contains five windows on each side, each window being placed over one of the piers of the nave arcading.

During the Early English period, probably by John de Berwick, who was dean from 1286 — 1312, a spire was added to the central tower. This was for long in an unsafe condition, and at length, in 1600, it fell. The following is the description given by Coker, a contemporary writer: "Having discoursed this longe of this church, I will not overpasse a strange accident which in our dayes happened unto it, viz. Anno Domini 1600 (the choire beeing then full of people at tenne of clock service, allsoe the streets by reason of the markett), a sudden mist ariseing, all the spire steeple, being of a very great height, was strangely cast downe, the stones battered all the lead and brake much timber of the roofe of the church, yet without anie hurt to the people; which ruin is sithence commendablie repaired with the church revenues, for sacriledge hath not yet swept awaye all, being assisted by Sir John Hannam, a neighbour gentleman, who if I mistake not enjoyeth revenues of the church, and hath done commendablie to convert part of it to its former use." Other accounts mention a tempest at the time of the fall. It is not unlikely that the tower was weakened by the alterations in the fourteenth century, when wider arches were cut in the west walls of the transepts, in consequence of the widening of the nave aisles. The fall of the spire, which fell towards the east, demolished the clerestory windows of the choir on the south side, and their place was supplied by a long, low Tudor window oblong in shape and quite plain. The windows, however, on both sides have been entirely altered, and those now existing in the clerestory are small lancets of modern date.

The spire was not rebuilt, but the heavy looking battlement and solid pinnacles which still remain, and detract considerably from the beauty of the tower, were added as a finish to it in the year 1608. It is curious that the churchwardens' books, in which many entries occur detailing repairs and other work connected with the spire, make no mention of its fall.

The western tower was also a source of trouble. It was built, as has been already mentioned, during the latter half of the fifteenth century, the glazing of the windows being completed in 1464; but as early as 1548 it was thought necessary to brick up the west doorway, and notices of unsoundness of the tower occur frequently in the church books. In 1664 we find the following entry made :—" Paid in beere to the Ringers for a

£ s d

peale to trye if the Tower shooke o 1 o." As we read this entry, we cannot help wondering if the large amount of beer which a shilling would purchase in those days was given to the ringers so as to give them a fictitious courage and blind their eyes to the possible danger of bringing the tower down upon their heads. In 1739 the Perpendicular window in the western face of the tower was taken out and a smaller oval one put in its place, with a view to the strengthening of the wall by additional stonework. The modern restorer, however, has again put a window of Perpendicular character in place of the oval window inserted in the last century, using to aid him in his design, sundry fragments of the original tracery found embedded in the walls.

Before the nineteenth-century restorations, the pulpit, probably late sixteenth-century work, stood in the nave against the middle pillar on the north side, and the nave and choir were separated by a screen of three arches on which stood the organ. The central arch had doors. On either side of the choir were a set of canopied stalls : these canopies were removed in 1855 to make the chancel aisles available for a congregation. As the canopies interfered with both sight and sound, the floor of the choir was lowered to only three steps above the nave, and

WIMBORNE MINSTER IN THE EIGHTEENTH CENTURY.

From an old Print.

the stalls reduced to four on each side, with a view to make room for restoring the Norman steps indicated by traces on the wall under the floor, which led up to the high altar of the Norman church. The arrangement of steps was then three from the nave to the choir, four from the choir to the next level to the east, and seven from this to the presbytery, and one more to the altar platform. In 1866 further changes were made : the remaining stalls were taken away, and the present seats for the choir and the reading-desk were manufactured out of the old woodwork. The level of the floors was also rearranged; five steps now lead up from the nave to the choir, seven to the presbytery and one more to the altar platform, the altar itself being raised yet another step.

During the restoration carried on from 1855 to 1857, great changes besides those already mentioned were made in the interior: the whitewash and plaster were removed from the walls, a west gallery was taken down, the nave re-seated, the organ transferred from its position upon the screen to the south transept, and much mischief was done from an archæological standpoint, a thing which seems almost inseparable from any nineteenth-century restoration.

An examination of the masonry shows clearly that all the exterior walls east of the transepts save the east wall of the presbytery, which is somewhat out of the vertical, the top hanging forward, have been if not entirely rebuilt at anyrate completely refaced, and this work was no doubt done at the restoration at the middle of the nineteenth century. The doorway in the middle of the north choir aisle is entirely modern ; the doorway which formally occupied this place was provided with a small porch.

How far this rebuilding and refacing were rendered necessary by the condition of the walls at that time it is now impossible to say. The fact that the walls of the nave aisles were not similarly treated may have been due to want of funds, or it may be that the architects employed found them in a better condition than the walls of the choir aisles, and so preserved them, though they considered the latter beyond the possibility of preservation without the extensive renewing that evidently took place.

The room containing the chained library was at the same

time refitted. New shelves and rods were provided, but the old chains were used again.

The restoration of 1855—1857 did not extend to the transept; but these were taken in hand in 1891, with the usual result—namely, the destruction of some existing features, such as the seventeenth-century tracery of the north window, to make room for a nineteenth-century window in Decorated style, which, however, differs altogether from any window in the minster; the walls were raised about two feet and a roof of higher pitch put upon them, which necessitated alterations in the gables. A sundial which stood at the summit of the south gable was taken down, and this in 1894 was erected on a pillar built in the churchyard, a short distance from the south wall of the western tower. The transept previous to the restoration with the sun-dial on its gable is shown in the illustration on p. 19.

CHAPTER II

THE EXTERIOR

WIMBORNE MINSTER does not occupy a commanding position—
it stands on level ground, its two towers are not lofty, the
western only reaching the height of 95 feet and the central
84 feet—but it has the advantage of having an extensive churchyard both on the south side and also on the north, so that
from either side a good general view of the building may be
obtained. A street running from the east end of the church
towards the north gives the spectator the advantage of a still
more distant standpoint, from which the towers, transepts, choir,
and porch group themselves into one harmonious whole, the
long line of iron railings bounding the churchyard being the
only drawback. The first impression is that there is something wrong with the central tower; the plain heavy battlement,
with its four enormous corner-pinnacles, seems to overweight
the tower, and as each side of the parapet is longer than the
side of the tower below, the feeling of top-heaviness is increased. The central tower has no buttresses, but the western
has an octagonal buttress at each corner, and these decrease
in cross section at each of four string courses; so that this
tower seems to taper, and by contrast makes the central tower
seem to bulge out at the top more than it really does.

But Wimborne Minster does not stand alone in giving at first
sight a feeling that something is wanting to perfect beauty.
In nearly every old building which has gradually grown up,
been altered and enlarged by various generations as need arose,
each generation working in its own style, and often with little
regard to what already existed, incongruities are sure to be
discernible. But what is lost in unity of design increases the
interest in the building, historically and architecturally regarded. And it is worthy of notice that at Wimborne, more
than at many places, the enlargers of the church have con-

16

tented themselves with adding to the building without removing the work of their predecessors more than was absolutely necessary. A very cursory glance at the exterior of the building as one walks round it is sufficient to show that the church as it stands offers to the student of architecture examples of every style that has prevailed in this country from the twelfth century onward, and he will especially rejoice at seeing so much fourteenth-century work. He will, as he passes along the narrow footway beneath the east end of the choir, regret that more space is not available here to get a good view of the most interesting Early English window. If a small tree were felled, and the wall of a garden or yard on the side of the footpath opposite to the church pulled down, so as to throw open the east end of the choir, it would be a great improvement. But this regret can be endured, as, though the window cannot be well seen, it is there, and by changing one's position a pretty accurate idea of its interesting features can be formed; but far keener is the regret that any lover of antiquity must feel when he notices, as he examines the church more closely, how busy the nineteenth-century restorer has been, how he has raised walls, altered the pitch of roofs, and inserted modern imitations of thirteenth and fourteenth century work, removing features which existed at the beginning of this century to make room for his own work; how he has banished much of the old woodwork in the interior, altered the position of still more, and generally been far less conservative of the work of former generations than the mediæval enlargers of the minster were. However, his work is now done—nave, towers, and choir were thoroughly restored about fifty years ago, and the transepts in 1891. No further work is contemplated at present. In fact, there seems nothing more that could well be done.

The church is built partly of a warm brown sandstone, partly of stone of a pale yellow or drab colour, the two kinds being in many places mixed so as to give the walls a chequered appearance. This may be noticed both outside and inside the building. In some of the walls the stones are used irregularly, in others they are carefully squared. The red stone is to be met with in the neighbourhood: some of that used for raising the transept walls in 1891 was obtained from a bridge in the town that was being rebuilt; and from marks on

B

some of those stones it appeared that before being in the bridge they had been used in some ecclesiastical building, so that they have now returned to their original use. There is little ornament to be seen outside, save on the upper stage of the tower; in fact, the whole building excepting the arches of the nave and the tower may be described as severely plain in character. The college was never wealthy, hence probably it could not employ a number of carvers; then again it was not a monastic establishment, so that there were no monks to occupy their time in the embellishment of the building, carving, as monks often did, their quaint fancies on bosses and capitals. We miss the crockets and finials, the ball-flower, and other ornaments that we meet with in so many fourteenth-century buildings; but the very simplicity of the work gives the church a dignity that is often wanting in more highly ornamented structures. The small number of the buttresses in the body of the church is noteworthy; save at the angles there are only five—namely, two on each nave aisle, and one on the north choir aisle. At each of the eastern corners of the choir aisles the buttresses are set diagonally, as also are those on the northern corners of the north porch. There is a buttress on each of the side walls of the north porch, and two set at right angles to each other at each of the two corners of the north transept, and also at the south-west corner of the south transept; beneath the east window of the choir there is a small one. The buttresses at the corner of the choir project but slightly. The central tower has none, but the west tower has an octagonal buttress at each corner. The central tower attracts notice first. From the outside at the angles a small portion of the plain wall of the triforium stage may be seen, against which the roofs of the choir and transepts abut; the nave roof, however, hides all of this stage at the western face: above this face is a band of red-brown sandstone, and above this the clerestory stage. In each face are two round-headed windows with a pointed blank arch between them. There are six slender shafts to support the outer order of moulding over the two windows and the blank arch, and two of a similar character to support the inner ring of moulding over each window. At each corner of the tower up to the top of this stage runs a slender banded shaft. This stage is finished by a string course, above which

THE MINSTER FROM THE SOUTH-EAST BEFORE 1891.

the tower walls recede slightly, the walls of the upper or belfry storey being a little thinner than those below. This stage, perfectly plain within, is the most richly-ornamented part of the tower outside : it is the latest Norman work to be found in the minster, and probably may be dated late in the twelfth century. An arcading of intersecting round-headed arches runs all round this storey. Seven pointed arches are thus formed in each face ; between these arches stand slender pillars with well carved capitals which show a great variety of design. Five of the seven arches on each face were originally open, save possibly for louvre-boards placed to keep out the rain; now all but the central one on each face are walled up, and the centre one is glazed. This filling up was not all done at the same time, as the varying character of the stone shows. The work was no doubt begun in order to strengthen the walls when the spire was added, and was continued from time to time as the necessity for further strengthening arose. Above the stage was a bold corbel table, and this is the upper limit of the Norman work. There can be little doubt that the Norman builder, here as elsewhere, finished his tower with a low pyramidal roof with overhanging eaves to shoot off the rain. This covering may have been of lead, but possibly of stone tiles or wooden shingles. About a century later this Norman roof was removed to make place for a loftier roof or spire. Of its character and material and height we know nothing—there is no description of it ; and though the minster is represented on an old seal with one spire-crowned tower, yet the representation of the rest of the church is so conventional that it cannot be regarded as an authentic record of the actual appearance of the steeple. It is curious that, as it stood for about three hundred years and fell only in the later years of Elizabeth's reign, no drawing remains to show us what this spire was like. But it passed away, doing some damage to the building in its fall, and that is the only record it has left behind ; but we can well picture to ourselves how much importance must have been added to the minster by this spire, which must have been a conspicuous object for many miles round. The present heavy, ugly battlemented parapet spoils the general effect of the tower ; and though we are adverse to the sweeping away of any features of an old building, even when the features are inharmonious and even ugly—because this is, as it were, tearing a

THE NORTH TRANSEPT BEFORE 1891

page of stone from the book of the history of the building—
yet we must confess we could have regarded the loss of the
seventeenth-century parapet and pinnacles with much less
regret than other features which the restorer has tampered
with.

The **North Porch,** which was evidently always intended to
be, as it is to this day, the chief entrance into the church, consists
of two bays marked externally by buttresses on each side : the
inner order of moulding to the arch giving access to this porch
springs from two shafts of Purbeck marble ; the outer orders
are carried up from the base without any capitals or imposts.
The height of the crown of the inner arch above the capitals
from which it springs is somewhat less than half the width
at the bottom, and the radius of the curvature of the arches
is greater than the width. Over the arch is a square-headed two-
light window, lighting the room over the entrance. The roof
differs from all the other roofs of the church since it is covered
with stone tiles, while the others are covered with lead. There
are buttresses set diagonally at the two northern angles of the
porch.

Between the porch and the transept are three two-light
Decorated windows. The tracery of all these is alike, but
differs from that of the two windows to the west of the porch.
The most picturesque feature of the north transept is the turret
containing the staircase by which access is obtained to the
tower. This, before the church was enlarged in the fourteenth
century, formed the north-west angle of the Norman transept :
projecting towards the north, its base is rectangular. This
rectangular portion rises nearly to the level of the tops of the
aisle windows, above this level the turret is circular, and rising
above the transept roof is capped by a low conical roof of
stone tiles. Two string courses run round it, one at the
bottom of the circular part, and one a little higher up. This
turret was once known as the "Ivy Tower," from the ivy that
grew on it, but this was all removed at the time when the
transept was altered in 1891. At that time the side walls were
raised about two feet, and the roof was raised to the original
pitch of the Norman transept, and at the same time the tracery
of the north window, which was of a very plain and clumsy
character, seventeenth-century work, was removed and the
existing tracery inserted. Much picturesqueness has been

sacrificed to make these changes. The portion of this transept to the north of the turret was added about the middle of the fourteenth century to form the chantry founded by Bembre, who was dean from 1350—1361. This part contains, besides the large window, two smaller two-light windows, which look out respectively to the east and west. The tracery in these is almost entirely modern. Beyond the transept is the wall of the north choir aisle. This stands farther to the north than the wall of the nave aisle ; in fact, it is in a line with the original north end of the Norman transept. In this wall, close to the transept, is a small round - headed doorway. And, farther to the east, is another larger pointed doorway between the second and third windows of the choir aisle, counting from the transept eastward. This doorway is enclosed by a triangular moulding very plain in character, but none of it is original. The three windows are each of two lights. The tracery of these three is alike, but differs from that of the windows in the nave aisle. The east window of the north aisle is of five lights. The enclosing arch is not very pointed — much less so than in the narrower windows of the aisles—and each light runs up through the head of the window. These and the

THE EAST WINDOW.
(From Parker's " Introduction to Gothic Architecture.")

corresponding south choir aisle windows are late Decorated work.

Unfortunately the churchyard does not extend to the east of the church. A narrow footway, bounded to the east by cottages and garden walls, renders it impossible to photograph the east window of the choir. This is a most interesting one ; and has been figured in most books on architecture. It consists externally of three lancets enclosed in a peculiar way by weather moulding ; this rises separately over the head of each lancet, and between the windows runs in a horizontal line and is continued to the square corner buttresses. Within this moulding, and over the heads of each lancet, there is an opening pierced : the central one is a quatrefoil, while the other two have six points. These openings are a very early example of plate tracery, which was fully developed in the Early Decorated style. This window belongs to the Early English period, and may be dated about 1220. There will be occasion to refer to this window again when speaking of the interior of the church. The south choir aisle has a five-light east window closely corresponding to the window of the north aisle, and on the south two three-light windows. In these, as in the east aisle windows, the lights are carried up through the heads. There is no doorway giving access to this aisle from the outside.

The angle between the choir aisle and south transept is filled up with the vestry and the library above it. The south wall of this projects beyond the wall of the south transept. This vestry is of Decorated date, possibly rather later than the other Decorated work in the minster. The upper storey forms the library. Its walls are finished at the top by a plain parapet which conceals the flat roof. At the south-western angle is an octagonal turret staircase, capped by a pyramidal roof rising from within a battlemented parapet, and terminating in a carved finial. This is of Perpendicular character. From the sharpness of the stone at the coigns it would seem that very extensive restoration, if not absolute rebuilding, of the walls was carried on in this part of the church. The south transept is rather shorter than that on the north side ; but, unlike it, all the walls up to the level of the window are of Norman date. The string courses on the western side are worthy of close attention. One which runs under the south window is continued round the Perpendicular buttresses at the south-west angle, and then again joins the original course on the western face and runs to within a few feet of the nave aisle, where it abruptly terminates. Above this for several feet the walls have the same character as below; then the character changes, and this change probably marks the junction of the Norman with the Decorated work, which was added when the Norman chapel, which occupied the lower part of what is now the south end of the transept, was incorporated in the transept. Vertically above the termination of the string course just mentioned, but at a considerably higher level, another string course abruptly begins and runs along the wall, until it passes within the roof of the nave aisle. The south end of this shows the length to which the original Norman transept extended before the walls of the chapel to the south were carried up in the fourteenth century to form the addition to the transept. In the southern wall of this new transept was placed a large five-light decorated window. In this, as in several of the other Decorated windows already described, the lights run up to the enclosing arch above. The tracery of this window, as it now exists, dates back only to the time when the church was restored in the middle of the nineteenth century. Up to 1891 the side walls were about two feet lower than at present, and the gable more obtuse. At the summit of the old gable stood a block of masonry carrying a sundial; this, when the transept was altered, was removed, the new gable being finished with a cross. A pillar was built in the churchyard to the south of the western tower in 1894, and on it the block from the transept bearing the sundial was placed. This sundial has two dates on it—1696 and 1752, marking, no doubt, the year of its original erection and of some subsequent repair. It is noteworthy that the figures used in these two dates differ in character,—the eighteenth-century carver who incised the later date not thinking it incumbent on him to make his figures match those of his predecessor. The three aisle windows between the south transept and the south porch are two-light Decorated windows with tracery, some of it original, corresponding to that of those on the opposite side in the north aisle.

The **South Porch** is small, and the side walls do not project

far from the aisle.　Above the arch is a carving of a lamb much
weathered, and on the gable stands a fragment of a cross.
The gates beneath the outer arch are kept locked save on
Sundays, as are frequently the gates in the railings surrounding
the churchyard to the south of the minster, which is divided from
the churchyard on the north side by the church itself and by railings at the east and west ends of it.　To the west of the porch are
two more two-light windows, corresponding in character with the
windows opposite in the north aisle.　The clerestory windows
of the nave are of Perpendicular date, fifteenth-century work,
and have not any beauty.　Each has three foliated lights
under a round-headed moulding.　Above each of these three
there are two lights, all enclosed within a rectangular label.
The nave roof is higher than the choir roof.　Its aisles have
lean-to roofs, whereas the choir aisles are wider and have
gable roofs : hence the clerestory windows of the choir, modern
lancets, are not visible from the outside.

The **Western Tower** is of four stages, with octagonal
buttresses at each corner, decreasing in cross section at
each course.　Of these the north-eastern one contains the
stairs leading to the top of the tower, the others are solid.
These are crowned with sharp pyramidal turrets.　In the
lowest stage on the western face is a doorway which for
some time was stopped up to strengthen the tower, but
which was opened again at the general restoration.　Above
this is the west window of six lights, Perpendicular in character but of nineteenth-century date.　The third stage—the
ringing room within is lighted by four small windows : that in
the west wall is a quatrefoil, those on the north and south
have single lights foliated at the head ; the original one in
the east wall was covered when the nave roof was raised, and
a plain opening was made in the wall farther to the south.
Above this is the belfry, with two pairs of two-light windows
on each face : these are divided by transoms, and the arches
at the tops are four centred.　These windows are, of course,
not glazed, but are furnished with louvre-boards.　The tower
is finished with a battlemented parapet.　Just outside the
easternmost window on the north face, and below the transom,
stands a figure now dressed in a coat of painted lead, representing a soldier in the uniform of the early part of the nineteenth
century.　He holds a hammer in each hand, with which he

THE WESTERN TOWER.

strikes the quarters on two bells beside him.   He is known by
the name of the "Jackman" or "Quarter Jack."   There are
no windows at the west ends of the nave aisles ; but, as on the
south side so on the north, there are between the tower and
the porch two two-light Decorated windows in the wall of the
aisle.

The level of the churchyards, as in the case with most old
burying-grounds, is considerably above the level of the floor
of the church.   Hence steps have to be descended on entering
the porches, and again in passing from the porches into the
church.   On the south side some levelling of the ground has
been done, and the upright head-stones have been laid flat,
but the altar tombs have been allowed to remain as they
were.   There are few trees in the churchyard to impede the
view of the building; those there are, are as yet small, and
serve only to pleasantly break the bareness of the ground
without hiding the architectural features of the building.

CHAPTER III

THE North Porch, which no doubt from the days of its erection in the fourteenth century has formed the chief entrance into the church, is opposite to the westernmost Norman bay of the nave arcading. The porch itself is vaulted in two bays, the vaulting springing from slender shafts of Purbeck marble which rest on the stone seats on either side of the porch. The bosses in which the ribs meet are carved with foliage. Over the porch is a small room to which no staircase now leads ; one which formerly led to it was removed in the seventeenth century. This room is lighted by a small two-light Decorated window facing north.

The two **Aisles** are of the same length as the nave, and are divided from it by an arcading on either side, each containing six pointed arches. The easternmost arches consist of two plain orders, and are much narrower than the rest. These arches spring on the east side from brackets on the western face of the tower piers : the bracket on the north side is plain, that on the south side is ornamented with a kind of scale carving. These bays were probably of the same date as the tower, and it is not unlikely that the arches were at first like those of the tower, of the usual round-headed form. If they were altered when the remainder of the nave was built, the wall above was not removed. The piers which support the western side of these arches consist each of a semi-cylindrical pillar set against a rectangular pier, on the other side of which another semi-cylindrical shaft is set to support the next arch ; the next two pillars on each side are cylindrical, perfectly plain in the shafts with very simple bases and capitals. The latter may be seen in the illustrations, the former are concealed by the pews. It will be noticed as a peculiar feature that a little piece of the outer moulding, facing the nave, of the first large arch on the south

29

THE INTERIOR, LOOKING EAST.

side is differently carved from all the rest : first, counting from
the bottom upwards, are three eight-leaved flowers—these are
succeeded by three four-leaved flowers, all on a chamfered
edge ; above this the moulding is not chamfered, and the outer
face is decorated with shallow zig-zag carving. The second

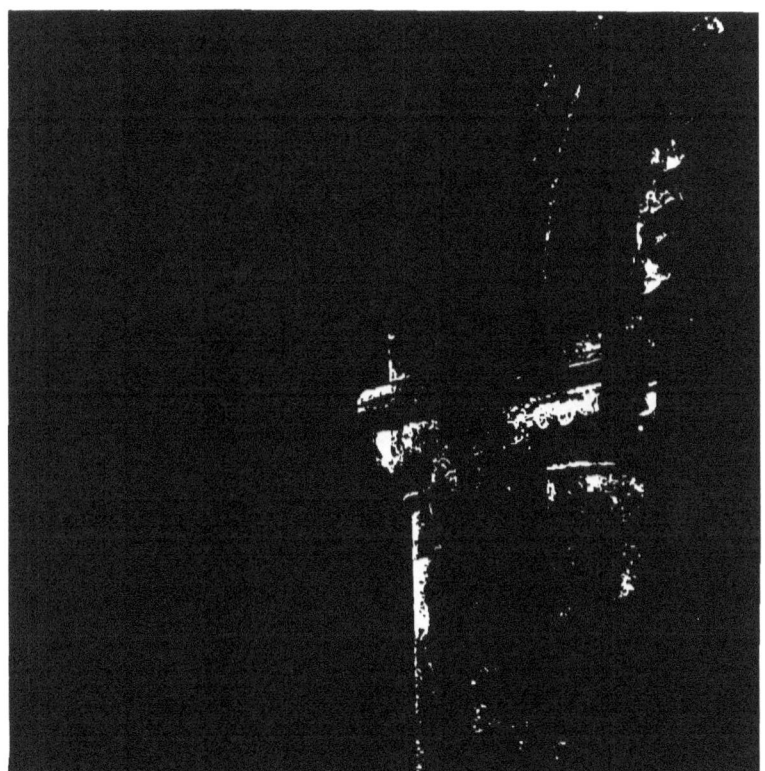

PIER AND ARCH-SPRING IN THE SOUTH ARCADE.

member of the moulding consists of chevron work somewhat
irregularly carved, the projecting tooth-like points not being
all of the same size ; in the centre is a roll moulding, from
each side of which chevron ornamentation projects, the points
directed outward perpendicular to the plane of the arch.

These pillars and arches are noteworthy in that the piers are of considerable size, and above them are pointed arches.   This would indicate a rather late date in the

DECORATED ARCH IN THE NAVE.

Norman period for this portion of the church; probably it was built at some time during the last quarter of the twelfth century.   With the third wide bay the twelfth-century church

terminated, the two arches to the west of these being character-
ised by ornamentation of the Decorated period. At this time,
as has been already explained (p. 10), the aisles were widened
and the inner edges of the roofs raised above the clerestory
windows of the Norman church. Four such windows, round-
headed, each placed over the point of an arch, may be seen on
either side of the nave ; but the eastern one on each side differs
from the other three in being of heavier character and rougher
workmanship. The external mouldings of these can be well
seen from the aisles : towards the nave they are splayed and
plain. The wall above the fourteenth-century arches does not
contain any windows on the same level as those of the old
Norman clerestory ; but above them, stretching all along each
side of the nave, may be seen the windows of the present
clerestory. These are Perpendicular in style, and are five in
number on each side, each window being placed over one of
the piers of the nave arcading. These windows are square-
headed, and have at the bottom three lights, each light being
sub-divided into two at the top. It is believed that this
clerestory was formed when the walls were raised, at the
same time as the western tower was erected namely, at the
end of the fifteenth century. But to return to the Decorated
arches at the west end of the nave. The pier at the eastern
side of the easternmost of these consists of the semi-cylindrical
respond of Norman date, a piece of masonry which was part of
the west wall of the Norman church ; and then on the western
side of this an added semi-cylinder, on the capitals of which
may be seen the ball-flower ornament. The pier on either side,
between the two fourteenth-century arches, is octagonal, with
a very plain capital (one of these is shown in the illustration on page 57) ; the arches themselves are also plain,
consisting of two members with chamfered edges. The half
pillars at the western side of the western arch have been
imbedded in the octagonal buttresses of the west tower,
which project into the church.

The height of the nave roof appears to have been altered on
several occasions. There may be seen from the interior of
the nave, on the west wall of the lantern tower, two lines
running from the level of the tops of the Norman clerestory
windows : these make an angle of about forty-five degrees with
the horizontal, and, no doubt, are traces of the weather mould-

c

ings marking the position of the exterior of the roof of the nave in Norman times. Probably the roof visible from the interior was flat and formed of wood, and ran across in the line of the string course above the tower arch, at a level slightly above the heads of the clerestory windows. A round-headed opening above this string course probably gave admission to the space between the outer and inner roofs. At a somewhat higher level, we have a slight trace which probably marks the junction of the fifteenth-century roof with the tower. This roof was of oak and very plain—at the restoration the pitch of the roof was raised and carried up to such an extent as to cut off the bases of the clerestory windows of the lantern tower; the inner roof itself is of pitch-pine, with hammer-beams of the character which finds such favour with nineteenth-century architects.

The **Central Tower**, the oldest and probably most interesting part of the church, consists of four stages, of which the three lower ones are open to the church. The lowest of these was undoubtedly part of the original Norman church; the second or triforium was soon added. Above this comes the clerestory, the pointed arch between the round-headed windows indicating a somewhat later date; and above this there is a chamber perfectly plain within, and not open to the church below. The outside of this is decorated with an arcading of intersecting arches, which indicates a somewhat later date. These intersecting arches form seven pointed arches on each side—five of these were originally open to allow the sound of the bells, which were formerly hung in the tower, to pass out; but to add strength to the walls all but the middle ones on the east face were at various periods walled up. At one time the tower was surmounted by a spire, possibly of wood covered with lead; this is supposed to have been erected by John de Berwick, who was dean of the minster from 1286 to 1312. The squinches which supported this spire may still be seen in the upper stage just described. Descending from this stage by a spiral staircase in the north-west angle, we find ourselves in the clerestory already mentioned. In each face there are two round-headed windows widely splayed on the interior, with shafts in the jambs; between each pair of windows is a pointed arch, in each angle of the tower is a slender shaft encircled by three bands at about equidistant intervals: a passage cut in the thickness of the wall runs round this stage. Again descending, we reach the triforium level. Each of the walls of this stage has two pointed sustaining arches built into the wall to support the weight of the superincumbent masonry ; each of these encloses four semi-circular headed arches with shafts of Purbeck marble. The capitals of these are rudely carved, and between the relieving pointed arches are carved heads, that on the north side being the most noteworthy. The passage behind the arches is very narrow, the total thickness of the walls being

CLERESTORY STAGE OF THE CENTRAL TOWER.

only 4 feet 6 inches. At the centre of each face are the openings which formerly led into the spaces between the roofs and ceilings of the nave, transepts, and choir of the Norman church. That on the north side now leads into a stone gallery, erected in 1891 in the place of a dilapidated wooden structure, which runs first westward to the angle between the tower and north transept, then along the west face of the transept until it reaches a door leading into the stair turret, which may be seen from the exterior. At the bottom of this is a door opening into the transept. This stair turret projects

THE TOWER ARCHES.

slightly into the transept. The lowest stage of the tower consists of four arches and four massive piers. The arches

NORTH TRANSEPT AND CROSSING

have two plain orders. The piers have double shafts supporting the central order, and single shafts supporting the outer
orders. The four arches are not of the same width, those on
the east and west being wider than those on the north and
south. In order to get the arches to spring from the same
level and also to reach the same height at their heads, the
wider arches are of the shape known as "depressed," while
the narrower ones are of the "horse-shoe" type. The choir
being somewhat narrower than the nave, the walls on each
side take the place of the shaft which would have supported
the outer order of the eastern arch. The capitals and bases of
these arches are very plain, in fact nowhere in this church
can the elaborately-carved capitals so often met with in late
Norman work be found. This central tower was undoubtedly
gradually raised stage by stage, as the character of the
architecture indicates: probably during each interval the
part already finished was capped by a pyramidal roof.

The **Nave Aisles** were widened in the fourteenth century,
the Norman walls being removed and their roofs raised; a single
stone of the weather moulding, which may be seen on the west
face of the north transept, shows the height and slope of the
roof of the Norman aisle. The windows of the aisles on
either side are two-light Decorated windows; the three on
either side to the east of the north and south porches are of
the same character, while the two on each side to the west of
the porches are also alike but differ in their tracery from those
to the east. The south porch is much smaller than the north,
and is very plain; it is composed of two solid walls projecting
six feet from the wall of the aisle.

The **Transepts,** as has been described in the preceding
chapter, were lengthened in the fourteenth century — the
southern one by the incorporation of some low Norman
building, thought by some to have been the Lady Chapel,
the walls of which were raised; the northern one by the
addition of Bembre's chantry. This has caused the north
transept to be somewhat longer than the south. The original
Norman transepts seem to have been of the same length
on either side. Bembre, who died in 1361, is supposed
to have been buried here. A stone slab lay until 1857 in
the centre of the pavement,—on it was a representation of a
full-length figure of a man dressed in a robe like a surplice;

but when the pavement was renewed this stone was allowed to remain exposed to sun and rain in the churchyard until the surface was weathered to such an extent that it is now impossible to make out with any certainty what is upon it. But the description given by Hutchins of the arms on the shields which were sculptured on it does not agree with the Bembre arms, so that it could hardly have been the tombstone of this Dean who founded the chantry. The window at the end of the north transept is modern restoration work. Before 1891 the tracery was of a very plain character, as may be seen from the illustration (page 21). It is supposed that damage was done to this window at the time when the tower fell, and that the plain tracery was inserted after that event. During the restoration in 1891, the old plaster was removed from the walls, and in doing this a Norman altar recess was discovered in the east wall of this transept ; the southern end of this had been cut away when the choir aisle was widened in the fourteenth century. In this recess traces of fresco may be seen.

THIRTEENTH-CENTURY PISCINA IN SOUTH TRANSEPT.

A piscina stands to the north of this altar recess, and is of Decorated character.

The **South Transept** has a five-light Decorated window at its southern end, with modern tracery in imitation of the old,

each light running up through the head of the window.   A
very fine Early English piscina, with the characteristic dog-
tooth moulding, stands in the south wall.   An altar occupying
a position similar to the one in the north transept used to

CHOIR STALLS.

stand in this transept also, but the pointed arch over the
recess shows that it was of later date.

The most elaborate part of the church is that which lies
to the east of the central tower. The great height to which
the altar is raised above the level of the nave gives it a
very impressive appearance from the west end; and, again,

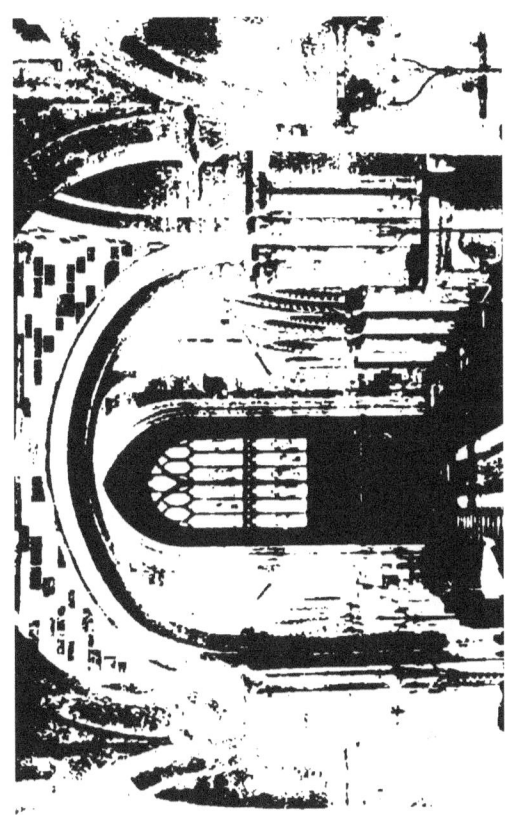

the view looking westward from the altar level is much enhanced by the height from which it is seen.

The **East End** is purely English work, and this shows that in the thirteenth century the church was extended about 30 feet towards the east. The junction of the Early English with the Norman wall is marked by a cluster of slender shafts rising from the ground. The alterations which were made in the Norman walls at the time of this eastward extension have been already described (p. 11).

It now only remains to describe the **Choir** and **Presbytery** as they stand at the present time. Immediately to the east of the tower on either side are two pointed arches of two plain orders rising on their western sides from plain brackets in the tower piers, and supported on the east by engaged shafts with roughly-carved Norman capitals. Next to these come the Early English inserted arches, pierced as already described through the Norman wall and cutting away the lower part of two previously existing Norman windows on each side. The arches are of three plain orders, with chamfered edges, resting on clustered shafts; beyond these the new thirteenth - century work begins. Beyond the clustered shafts mentioned above, which mark the commencement of the Early English work, is a lofty arch on either side opening into the choir aisles; over each of them is a pair of small lancet windows widely splayed inside. Between the piers of these arches a wall is carried, its top being about midway between their bases and capitals. On the southern wall stands the Beaufort tomb, on the northern the Courtenay tomb; and below this the walls are pierced with arches, beneath which are flights of nine steps leading on to the crypt beneath the presbytery. It is not improbable that after the eastern extension the altar stood at the east end of the Norman part of the choir, and that under these two Early English arches was the ambulatory or processional passage which is so often found to the east of the high altar. Beyond the ends of the choir aisles on either side of the presbytery is a lancet window. The east window is worthy of the closest observation. Its exterior appearance has been already described (p. 24). Within, it consists of three openings widely splayed; the thin stone over the central lancet, beneath the surrounding moulding, is pierced with a quatrefoil opening;

over the two side lancets the corresponding openings have
six foliations; between the three lights and outside the outer
ones, flush with the wall, are clusters of shafts of Purbeck

THE EAST WINDOW.

marble, from which spring mouldings enclosing the lights
in a most peculiar fashion : these follow the curves of the
tops of the lancets, but before meeting they are returned in
the form of cusps, and then are carried round the upper

foliated openings.   The upper part of each of these mouldings forms about three-quarters of the circumference of a
circle.   The characteristic Early English dog-tooth ornament
is carved round the moulding of the central light, those
round the other lights are not thus decorated.   The whole
group is surrounded by a label following the curves of
moulding, with carved heads at its terminations and points
of junction.   The six cusps of the moulding are ornamented
by bosses of carved foliage.

SEDILIA.

To the south side of the presbytery, between the south
window and the Beaufort tomb, the triple **Sedilia** and the
Piscina are situated : each of these is covered by a canopy
of fourteenth-century work.   These were extensively repaired
at the time of the restoration.   The Beaufort altar tomb is
the finest monument in the church.   On it are two recumbent
figures carved in alabaster, and although there is no inscription it is certain that they represent John Beaufort, Duke of

Somerset, and his wife Margaret. John Beaufort was son of another John Beaufort, Earl of Somerset, who was brother of the celebrated Cardinal Beaufort, and son of John of Gaunt by his mistress Catherine Swynford, a family afterwards legitimatised by Parliament. This second John Beaufort distinguished himself in the French wars of Henry IV., who in 1443 gave him a step in the peerage, creating him Duke of Somerset. His wife Margaret was, when he married her, widow of Oliver St John, and it is

THE BEAUFORT TOMB.

thought that after the death of her second husband in 1444 she married again. This John and Margaret, Duke and Duchess of Somerset, are famous on account of their daughter the Lady Margaret, so well-known for her educational endowments and for the fact that after her marriage with Edmund Tudor, the Earl of Richmond, she became the mother of that Henry Tudor who overthrew Richard III. at Bosworth, and was crowned King as Henry VII. Here on this altar tomb their effigies remain in a wonderful state of preservation, their right hands clasped together, angels at their heads, his feet resting on a dog, hers on an antelope. He is completely clad in armour, the face and right hand only bare—the gauntleted left hand holds the right hand gauntlet, which he has taken off that he may hold the lady's hand. She is clad in a long close-fitting garment. Each of the two wears around the neck a collar marked with the letters SS. At the apex of the arch above their tomb hangs his tourney helm.

Under the corresponding arch on the opposite side is a similar tomb, but without any effigy. The fragment of an inscription tells us that it is the tomb of one who was once the wife of Henry Courtenay, Marquis of Exeter, and mother of Edward Courtenay. She was Gertrude, daughter of William Blount, Lord Mountjoy. Her husband was beheaded in 1538, together with the aged Margaret, Countess of Salisbury, whose chantry may be seen in the Priory at Christchurch, though she was laid to rest in what Macaulay describes as the saddest burying-ground in England, the cemetery of St Peter's, in the Tower. Gertrude, Lady Courtenay, was herself attainted at the time of her husband's execution, but was afterwards pardoned and died in 1557. The tomb was opened in the last century from idle curiosity, and some one attempted to raise the body to a sitting posture, with the result that the skeleton fell to pieces. The tomb was also damaged by this foolish opening.

BRASS OF ÆTHELRED.

Three small carved figures at the bottom of the hood moulding of the arches over these monuments deserve attention. The one on the west side of the southern arch represents Moses with the tables of the law. Probably there was another such figure at the eastern end of the same moulding, but this would have been cut away when the sedilia were inserted. The opposite arch has a figure on each side.

Just at the east end of the Courtenay tomb is a slab of Purbeck marble, reputed to have once covered the grave of Æthelred. In it is inserted a fifteenth-century brass, with a rectangular plate of copper bearing an inscription, represented in the illustration (p. 46). A brass plate with a similar inscription, though the date on it is given as 872, was found in the library. Possibly the original brass and inscription were taken up in the time of the civil wars and hidden for safety, and the inscription having been lost, the copper plate now on the tomb was made when the brass was replaced, and the original plate was afterwards found and was placed for safety in what is now the library. *Copper* nails were used to fasten the brass to the floor, which perhaps serves to show that the engraved *copper* plate was made at the time when the brass was replaced on the slab. A little piece of the left-hand bottom corner has been broken off, and the top of the sceptre is missing. There are no rails before the altar, but their place is supplied by three oak benches covered with white linen cloths (these may be seen in the illustration on p. 43). The use of the "houseling linen" dates back to very early times. The word "housel" for the sacrament of the Lord's Supper has gone out of use, though most of us are familiar with the line

" *Unhouseled*, unanointed, unanelled,"

in which the ghost of Hamlet's father describes the circumstances of his death. The word "unhouseled" in this means that he died without receiving the sacred elements before his death.

The benches are a relic of Puritan times: there is an entry dated 1656 in the churchwardens' accounts respecting the payment of £1 "for making and setting up the benches about ye communion table in the quire." These were at first used as seats, on which the communicants sat to receive the bread and wine. In after times their use was modified. These benches, ten in number, were placed on the steps leading up to the altar, and it was customary for the clerk on "Sacrament Sundays" to go to the lectern after morning prayer, and, in a loud voice, give notice thus: "All ye

who are prepared to receive the Holy Communion draw near."
Those who wished to communicate then went into the chancel
and sat on these benches or in the choir stalls, waiting their
turns, and kneeling on mats until the clergy brought them
the bread and wine. Up to 1852 there was a rail on the
top step, at the entrance of the presbytery, on which the
houseling linen hung. The rail, which was of no great
antiquity, was removed at that date, and three of the oak
benches were retained to supply its place; these are now
used as an ordinary communion rail, but are always covered
with the "fair white cloths."

The **South Choir Aisle,** known as the Trinity Aisle, has
at its east end a five-light window, each light of which runs up
through the head; the south wall is pierced by two three-
light windows of similar character. The wall opposite in
the western bay, against which the organ now stands, is blank,
as on the outside of this the vestry stands with the library
above it. At the east end of this aisle was the chantry
founded by the Lady Margaret, Countess of Richmond,
whose father and mother lie in the tomb already described
beneath the nearest arch on the north side of this aisle.
The altar of this chantry, as well as all the other altars in
the church, numbering ten in all, have been swept away,
no doubt at the time of the Reformation. But recently the
east end of this aisle has been fitted up with a communion
table for use at early services.

In this aisle is to be seen, under the second window from
the east, the marble or slate painted sarcophagus known as
the Etricke tomb. Anthony Etricke of Holt Lodge, Recorder
of Poole, was the magistrate who committed for trial the ill-
fated Duke of Monmouth, who, after his flight from Sedge-
moor, was captured in the north of Dorset near Critchell.
It is said that in his old age he became very eccentric, and
desired to be buried neither in the church nor out of it,
neither above ground nor under; and to carry out his wish
he got permission to cut a niche in the church wall, partly
below the level of the ground outside, and then firmly fixed in
it the slate receptacle which is now to be seen. Into this he
ordered that his coffin should be put when he died. Moreover, he had a presentiment that he should die in 1691, and
so placed that date upon the side of the sarcophagus. He,

however, lived twelve years longer than he expected, so that
when his death really occurred the date had to be altered to
1703. The two dates, the later written over the earlier, are
still to be seen. On the outside of the sarcophagus are
painted the arms of his family. The whole is kept in good
repair, for so determined was the good man that his memory
should be kept alive, and his last resting-place well cared for,
that he gave to the church in perpetuity the sum of 20s. per
annum,. to be expended in keeping the niche and coffin in
good order. When the church was restored in 1857 the outer
coffin was opened, and it was found that the inner one had
decayed, but that the dust and bones were still to be seen,

THE ETRICKE TOMB.

these were placed in a new chest and once more deposited in
the outer coffin.

In this aisle is also to be seen the relic chest, not formed as
chests usually are of wooden planks or slabs fastened together,
but hewn out of a solid trunk of oak. The chest is over 6 feet
long, but the cavity inside is not more than 22 inches in
length, 9 inches in width, and 6 inches in depth, hence it will
be seen how thick and massive the walls are. Originally it
contained the relics of the church, and probably is much older
than the present minster itself. It was afterwards used as a
safe for deeds. In 1735 some deeds were taken from it bearing
the date 1200.

Formerly, there stood on this aisle the tomb of John de

D

Berwick, dean of the college, who died in 1312. At his tomb once a year the parishioners met to receive the accounts of the outgoing churchwardens and to elect new ones. The altar tomb was removed about 1790, the slab at the top of it being let into the floor.

The **North Choir Aisle** is a foot narrower than the corresponding south aisle : it has three windows each with two lights instead of two of three lights. This is known as St George's aisle. In the east wall is a piscina of Perpendicular date. Two doors lead into this aisle—one at the corner, where the

RELIC CHEST.

walls of the aisle and transept meet, and one between the two easternmost windows. The principal objects in this aisle are two bulky chests, one containing the title-deeds of some charity lands in the parish of Corfe Castle. This is fastened by six locks, each of different pattern,—each trustee of the charity has a key, of his own special lock,—so that the chest can only be opened by the consent of the whole body. The other chest contains the parochial accounts ; this once had six locks, but now has only two.

In the south-eastern corner of this aisle lies a mutilated

effigy of a mail-clad knight with crossed legs. This is said to have been removed to the minster from another church when it was destroyed. Whom it represents is uncertain, but traditionally it is known as the Fitz Piers monument.

UVEDALE MONUMENT.

In this aisle is the monument of Sir Edmund Uvedale, who died in 1606. The monument was erected by his widow in "dolefull duety." It is in the Renaissance style, and was carved by an Italian sculptor. The old knight is represented clad in a complete suit of plate armour, though without a helmet. He lies on his right side, his head is raised a little from his right hand, on which it has been resting, as though he were just awaking from his long sleep, his left hand holds his gauntlet. Above the tomb hangs an iron helmet, such as was worn in Elizabethan times, and which very probably was once worn by Sir Edmund himself.

Between the eastern ends of the choir aisles, and beneath the eastern end of the presbytery, is the **Crypt**. This is a vaulted chamber, the vaulting being supported on two pairs of pillars, thus forming three aisles, as it were, running east and west, each containing three bays. The western bay is of somewhat later date than the central and eastern; the wall against which the westernmost of the pillars once stood was removed, but the piers were allowed to remain, backed up by a new piece of masonry built against them to support the new vaulting. The crypt is lighted by four windows, equal-sided spherical triangles in shape; two look out eastward, one northward beyond the chancel arch, one, correspondingly placed, to the southward. The centre of the east end is a blank wall. Against this the altar stood — a niche, probably a piscina, still may be seen. On each side of the place where the altar stood there are two openings into the choir aisles. The exteriors of these are of the same form and size as the crypt windows, but they are deeply splayed inside, and probably were used as hagioscopes or squints, to allow those kneeling in the choir aisles to see the priest celebrating mass at the crypt altar.

The **Vestry** stands in the south-east angle between the transept and choir aisle; it is a vaulted building dating from the fourteenth century, and is lighted by two windows, one looking to the east, the other to the south. A small door at the south-west corner opens upon the staircase leading to the **Library**—a chamber situated above the vestry. The collection consists chiefly of books left to the minster by will of the Rev. William Stone, Principal of New Inn Hall, Oxford, a native of Wimborne. They were brought from Oxford in 1686, under the care of the Rev. Richard Lloyd, at that time Master of the Grammar School at Wimborne. The books are chiefly works on divinity; some additions were subsequently and at various times made to the original collection. The books were attached

ENTRANCE TO CRYPT.

to the shelves for safety's sake by iron chains, the upper end
carrying rings which slid on rods fastened to the shelf above,
the other end to the edge of the binding of the books.   Hence
the volumes had to be placed on the shelves with their backs
to the walls.   The room in which the books were placed was
formerly known as the Treasury; it was refitted in 1857, but
the old chains are still used.   It would occupy too much space
were any attempt made to give a list of the books.   The oldest
volume is a manuscript of 1343, "Regimen Animarum,"

THE LIBRARY.

written on vellum, and containing a few illuminated initials.
A "Breeches," Black-Letter Bible, dated 1595, is another book
worth mentioning; also a volume of Sir Walter Raleigh's
History of the World.   A hole was burnt through 104 of its
pages.   It is said that Matthew Prior, the poet, was reading it
by candle light and fell asleep, and when he woke was much
distressed to find that the snuff from his candle had done the
mischief.   He did his best to repair the damage, by placing a

THE CRYPT.

tiny piece of paper over the hole in each page, and inserting the missing letters with pen and ink. The book has since been rebound, leaves taken from another copy having been bound in between the damaged pages.

THE FONT.

The lower part of the west tower is used as a baptistery; this is separated from the nave by a screen, formed of fragments of the old rood screen. In the centre stands the octagonal late Norman **Font**, supported by eight slender shafts of Purbeck marble, and a modern spirally-carved central pillar of white stone, through which runs the drain to carry off the water.

In the inner southern wall of this tower, rather low down, is fixed a curious old **Clock** made by Peter Lightfoot, a Glastonbury monk, in the early part of the fourteenth century. The earth is represented by a globe in the centre, the sun by a disc which travels round it once in twenty-four

THE CLOCK IN THE WEST TOWER.

hours, showing the time of day; the moon by a globe so fastened to a blue disc that it revolves once during a lunar month; half of this is painted black, the other half is gilt, and the age of the moon is indicated by the amount of the gilded portion visible—when the moon is full the whole of the gilt hemisphere is shown, when new the whole of the black. This clock still goes, the works being in a room in the tower above. It requires winding once a day. The same clock also causes the Jack outside the tower to strike the quarters.

In the **Belfry** is a peal of eight bells. The tenor weighs about 36 cwts., the treble 7 cwts.

The tenor bears this inscription :

> MR WILHEMUS LORINGE ME PRIMO FECIT,
> IN HONOREM STÆ CUTBERGÆ.
> RENOVABAR SUMPTU PAROCHALI PER AB,
> ANNO DOMINI 1629.

The seventh bell is dated 1798.

The sixth bell 1600, and is thus inscribed : "SOUND OUT THE BELLS, IN GOD REGOYCE."

The fifth 1698, "PRAISE THE LORD."

The fourth 1686, "PULSATA ROSAMUNDI MARIA VOCATA. SMV."

The third was originally the smallest bell of the peal, and bears the Latin hexameter : "SUM MINIMA HIC CAMPANA, AT INEST, SUA GRATIA PARVIS," and the words, "THIS BELL WAS ADDED TO YE FIVE IN 1686, Samuel Knight." The two smaller bells are of recent date.

The **Lectern** bears date 1623. The stone pulpit is modern (1868). The old wooden pulpit, whose place it has taken, has been removed to the church at Holt.

The earliest mention of an **Organ** is in 1405, but the earliest authentic record is of one set up by John Vaucks, Organ Master, in 1533. A memorandum in the church-wardens' accounts speak of him setting up a pair of organs on the rood loft. In the year 1643, we have records of the sale of organ-pipes and old tin. After the Restoration in 1664, we have a record of the purchase of a new organ for £180. This was repaired, enlarged, and rebuilt at various times, and at the restoration, when the rood screen was unfortunately destroyed, the organ was placed in the south choir aisle.

All the lower windows are now filled with painted glass; all of which, with the exception of a few fragments, is nineteenth-century work.

DEANS OF WIMBORNE

Martin Pattislee or Pattishull	appointed	1224
Ralph Brito	,,	1229
John Mansell	,,	1247
John de Kirkby	,,	1265
John de Berwick	,,	1286
Stephen de Mawley	,,	1312
Richard de Clare	,,	1312
Richard de Swinnerton	,,	1334
Richard de Merimouth	,,	1338
Richard de Kingston	,,	1342
Thomas de Clopton	,,	1349
Reginald de Bryan	,,	1349
Thomas de Bembre (founder of the chantry)	,,	1350
Henry de Buckingham	,,	1361
Richard de Beverley	,,	1367
John de Carp	,,	1398
Roger Tortington	,,	1408
Peter de Altebello	,,	1412
Walter Medford	,,	1416
Gilbert Kymer	,,	1427
Walter Herte	,,	1467
Hugh Oldham	,,	1485
Thomas Rowthel	,,	1508
Henry Hornby	,,	1509
Reginald Pole	,,	1517
Nicholas Wilson	,,	1537
COLLEGE DISSOLVED	,,	1547

CHAPTER IV

ABOUT a quarter of a mile to the north-west of Wimborne stands the chapel of **St Margaret's Hospital.** The date of the foundation of this hospital is uncertain; tradition has it that it was founded by John of Gaunt, son of Edward III., but this is without doubt wrong, as documents—the character of which seem to indicate an early thirteenth-century date — have been found, from which it appears that this hospital existed at that time, and was set apart for the relief and support of poor persons afflicted with leprosy. This disease was at one time so common in England that a great number of lazar-houses were erected in the country, and many were well endowed; but when, after a time, the disease became less violent, many abuses crept in, persons not really suffering from the disease pretended to be lepers in order to get pecuniary benefits, and hence in many cases the leper hospitals were suppressed, or converted to other purposes. At the present day we find in many places, as here at Wimborne, that they are used as almshouses.

This hospital, however, was not one of the well-endowed. It appears from a deed, dated in the sixteenth year of Henry VIII., that the hospital was chiefly maintained, not by endowments, but by the gifts of the charitable who were willing to contribute to its support; and to encourage the benevolent to give, the deed recites that "Pope Innocent IV., in the year 1245, by an indulgans or bulle did assoyl them of all syns forgotten, and offences done against fader and moder, and all swerynges neglygently made. This indulgans, grantyd of Petyr and Powle, and of the said pope, was to hold good for 51 yeres and 260 days, provided they repeated a certain specified number of Paternosters and Ave Marias daily." The date of this indulgence proves the antiquity of the hospital, as it shows that it was in existence before the middle of the thirteenth century. A

ST. MARGARET'S HOSPITAL.

chantry was also founded in the chapel here by John Redcoddes of one priest to say masses for his soul. To this chantry, according to a deed dated in the sixteenth year of Henry VI., many tenements in Wimborne belonged. In later times the Rev. William Stone, who has been mentioned before as the founder of the Minster Library, by his will left his lands and tenements in the parish of Wimborne Minster to be applied to the benefit of almsmen only who should live in St Margaret's Hospital.

There is a further endowment, but how it came to this hospital has not been discovered. The advowson and tithes of the Rectory of Poole were, in the reign of James I., granted to the Mayor and Corporation of Poole for forty years, on the corporation undertaking to find a curate to discharge the duties lately discharged by the vicar, and to pay a rent to the crown of £12, 16s. per annum. In the reign of Charles I., the advowson and tithes were granted to two men, Thomas Ashton and Henry Harryman, and their heirs for ever, on the same conditions; but they are now again held by the Corporation, who pay out of the revenues — to St Margaret's hospital £9, 16s.; to the churchwardens of Wimborne Minster, for the maintenance of the Etricke tomb, £1; and to the fellows of Queen's College, Oxford, to be spent in wine and tobacco on November 5th, yearly £2.

The Redcotte chantry possessed sundry vestments, the gift of Margaret Rempstone, in the thirty-fifth year of Henry VI., and plate, an inventory of which exists. This plate, on the dissolution of chantries, was given by the parishioners to the king, Edward VI. The hospital or almshouses stands on the high road from Wimborne to Blandford; the chapel joins one of the tenements occupied by the almsmen. These tenements are nine in number; three are inhabited by married couples, three by men, and three by women. Some of these cottages are of half timber, and thatched, others of modern brick. The chapel, at which there is now a service every Thursday afternoon, conducted by one of the minster clergy, is a plain building, which has been recently refitted, but remains, as far as windows and walls are concerned, in its original state. There are three doors in the north wall; the heads are pointed, and it is noteworthy that in the central door, that generally used for access to the chapel, the two sides of the arch are of different curvatures, so that the point of the arch is nearer to the right-hand side. The edge of the wall is chamfered round the doorways. The east window has a semicircular head, and plain wooden tracery dividing it into two lancet-headed lights with an opening above them. There is a window in both the south and north walls, near the east end, each of two lights; the south window is widely splayed inside; the head of each light has one cusp on each side. The head of each light of the north window has two cusps on each side. Farther to the west, on the south side, is a single narrow lancet, widely splayed, and still farther to the west is a semicircular opening with wooden tracery. The general character of the masonry would indicate that local workmen were employed in building this chapel, and that little was spent in ornamenting it at the time of the erection. There are, however, some traces of frescoes on the inside of the walls, both geometrical patterns and figures. The pointed doorways and the lancet window on the south side would indicate the thirteenth century as the date of the original building, and this agrees with the documentary evidence mentioned above for the foundation of the hospital. The roof is an open one of massive wooden rafters, with the beams running across at the level of the wall plates.

DIMENSIONS

Extreme length, exterior, E. to W.	198 feet
Extreme width, exterior, N. to S.	102 ,,
Length of Nave, interior	67 ,,
Width of Nave, interior	23 ,,
Height of Walls	40 ,,
Length of Nave Aisles, interior	70 ,,
Width of Nave Aisles, interior	13 ,,
Length of North Transept, interior	42 ,,
Width of North Transept, interior	18 ,,
Height of Walls, interior	30 ,,
Length of South Transept, interior	33 ,,
Width of South Transept, interior	18 ,,
Height of Walls	30 ,,
Length of Choir, interior	32 ,,
Width of Choir, interior	21 ,,
Height of Choir Walls	28 ,,
Length of Presbytery	30 ,,
Width of Presbytery	21 ,,

Length of North Choir Aisle	53	feet
Width of North Choir Aisle	21	,,
Length of South Choir Aisle	53	,,
Width of South Choir Aisle	20	,,
Length of Side of Central Tower (square), interior	31	,,
Height of Central Tower	84	,,
Length of Side of Western Tower (square), exterior	31	,,
Height of Western Tower	95	,,
Length of North Porch, N. and S., interior	15	,,
Width of North Porch, E. and W., interior	14	,,
Length of South Porch, N. and E., interior	6	,,
Width of South Porch, E. and W., interior	7	,,
Length of Vestry, N. and S., interior	15	,,
Width of Vestry, E. and W., interior	14	,,
Length of Baptistery, E. to W., interior	18	,,
Width of Baptistery, N. to S., interior	19	,,
AREA	10,725	sq. feet.

CHRISTCHURCH PRIORY

CHRISTCHURCH PRIORY, FROM THE BRIDGE.

CHRISTCHURCH PRIORY

CHAPTER I

HISTORY OF THE BUILDING

ON the promontory washed on the one side by the slow stream of the Dorset Stour, and on the other by the no less sluggish flow of the Wiltshire Avon, not far from the place where they mingle their waters before making their way amid mudflats and sandbanks into the English Channel, stands, and has stood for more than eight hundred years, the stately Priory Church which gives the name of Christchurch to a small town in the county of Hants. The massive walls of its Norman nave, its fifteenth-century tower, and its great length—for, from the east wall of its Lady Chapel to the west wall of its tower, it measures no less than 311 feet—make it a conspicuous object from the Channel, especially after sundown, when its form, rising above the low shore of Christchurch Bay, is silhouetted against the sky. It is one of the finest churches below cathedral rank that is to be found in England. It is a perfect mine of wealth to the student of architecture, containing examples of every style from its early, possibly Saxon, crypt to the Renaissance of its chantries. Here we may see the solid grandeur of Norman masonry in the nave, with its massive arcading and richly-wrought triforium; the graceful beauty of the Early English in its north porch and in the windows of the north aisle of the nave; the more fully developed Decorated in the windows of the south aisle of the same; and Perpendicular in the tower and Lady Chapel.

The crypts beneath the north transept and the presbytery may have belonged to the original church, but of that which is visible above ground the oldest part was due to Flambard, of whom more hereafter. When the first church was founded we cannot tell. Here, as in many other places, the origin is lost in the haze of antiquity and legend. Here, as at many other places, we find the original builders choosing one site, and the stones that they had laid during the day being removed by night by unseen, and therefore angelic, hands to another. It was on the heights of St Catharine, about a mile and a half away from the present site, that the human builders strove to raise their church. It may be that this hill, still marked by the ramparts of an ancient encampment, was not holy ground on account of its former occupation by heathens, though in after time, a chapel, built in the early part of the fourteenth century, existed there; but, anyhow, not on this hill, but on the flat lands of Saxon Tweoxneham, a name which passed into the forms of Thuinam and Twynham, that the great Priory Church was destined to stand. But not even when the human builders began to erect the church on the miraculously chosen ground did supernatural interposition cease. A stranger workman came and laboured at the building : never was he seen to eat as the other workmen did, never did he come with his fellows to receive his wages. Once, when a beam had been cut too short for the place it was to occupy, he lengthened it by drawing it out with his hand; and when the day for consecration came, and the other workmen gathered together to see their work hallowed by due ceremonial, this stranger workman was nowhere to be seen. The ecclesiastics came to the conclusion that this was none other than the carpenter's son of Nazareth, and the church which had in part been builded by the hands of the Christ Himself was fitly dedicated to Christ, and it still bears the name of Christchurch.

But, if we disregard these legends, we do not at once find ourselves on sure and certain ground. The foundation has been attributed to Æthelstan, but this is hardly likely, as, in a charter dated 939, he gives one of the weirs on the Avon at Twynham to the Abbey Church of Middleton, now Milton Abbey in North Dorset, which he would be hardly likely to do if he had founded, or were thinking of founding, a religious house at Twynham; and as he died in 940, not much time was left for any foundation after this grant. Again, we find King Eadred granting land and fishing near Twineham to Dunstan. However, in the time of the Confessor, mention is made of the canons of Holy Trinity possessing lands in Thuinam. It must be remembered that it had been intended, according to the legend, to dedicate the church to the Holy Trinity, and no doubt this was done, although it was also specially dedicated to the second Person. In Domesday the double name occurs. The canons of the Holy Trinity of Christchurch are said to hold lands in the village, and also in the Isle of Wight opposite. Certain it is that in the days of Eadward the Confessor there was a church at Twynham dedicated to the Holy Trinity, held by a dean and a college of secular canons. This church was swept away by Ranulf Flambard, the notorious justiciar and chaplain of William II., whose evil deeds, contrary to the oft-quoted passage from Mark Antony's speech in Julius Cæsar, are now generally forgotten; while the good deeds that he wrought,—the nave of this church, and the still grander nave of Durham Cathedral Church, Durham Castle, "Norham's castled steep," and Kepier Hospital, built while he held the most important diocese in the North of England,—live after him, and have shed a glory on his name. Evil he was in moral character without doubt, but a glorious builder nevertheless. Though he oppressed the clergy, though it was through his instrumentality and by his advice that sees were kept vacant for years, and when filled, only given to those who were able and willing to pay large sums to the king, yet it is rather as a great architect than as an ecclesiastic that we, who gaze with delight and admiration on his work that has come down to us, will regard him. It is said that, as his end drew nigh, he realised the amount of evil he had done, and strove to make his peace with heaven and restitution to some, at least, of those whom he had wronged. He died in 1128, and his body rests in the great Cathedral Church of St Cuthbert that he had done so much to raise. But it was in the earlier part of his career, before he received the bishopric of Durham in 1099, that he probably began the work at Christchurch with which we are at present concerned.* He was succeeded by Godric in 1099, who is called Senior and Patron and afterwards Dean; but Flambard seems still

* Sir Gilbert Scott, however, thought that the Norman nave of the Cathedral Church at Durham was commenced before Flambard became bishop, and that the new church at Christchurch was begun after that date, so that the work at Christchurch was copied by him from what he found already commenced at Durham when he went there.

to have exercised some authority over him, illegal probably, but none the less real. We find him granting to Godric, for the work of building, all the offerings made by strangers and pilgrims, and when a canon died his share of the revenues of the college was devoted to the same object, the vacancy not being filled up by the appointment of any new canon. Godric died after having been dean for a short time only, whereupon Henry I. appointed Gilbert de Dousgunels dean, having appropriated to himself the accumulated fabric fund. Henry I. granted the patronage of the church to Richard de Redvers, Earl of Devon, who appointed his chaplain, Peter, a Norman of Caen, dean. This dean seems to have diverted the funds from the work of completing the church, but his successor, Randulphus, carried on the work again, so that in his time the church and the conventual buildings were roofed in. In the time of Hilary, in the year 1150, the secular college of canons was converted into a Priory of Augustinian Canons. This change was made with the consent of Baldwin de Redvers, in accordance with the wishes of Henry of Blois, brother of King Stephen, and at that time Bishop of Winchester, who is well known from the fact of his founding the Hospital of St Cross, near Winchester. Hilary, two years before this change was made, had been consecrated Bishop of Chichester, and subsequently became one of the episcopal opponents of Thomas Becket. Henceforth, until the dissolution in the reign of Henry VIII., the head of the religious community at Christchurch was a prior, who was, according to a charter granted by Richard de Redvers in 1160, elected by the canons. There were, in all, twenty-six priors, and their names have come down to us, but with only the most meagre notices of the architectural work which was carried on by each of them. Extensive, however, it must have been; and from what we see of the church itself, it would seem as if building operations must have been almost constantly in progress.

In all probability there was, according to the usual plan of Norman churches, a tower at the junction of the nave and transepts, and beyond this an apsidal choir. But there is no documentary record of such a tower ever having been built or fallen, although its existence is rendered probable by a carving of a church with tower and spire on Draper's chantry, and by a similar representation on a seal, and in two other parts of the building. It is probable that the original choir extended westward beyond the transept, as at Westminster to the present day.

As has been stated above, the Norman church was commenced by Flambard towards the end of the eleventh century; and of the work so begun, the earliest existing remains are the arcading of the nave, the triforium, and the transepts with the eastern apsidal chapel attached to the south transept. Next to this in order came the walls of the aisles of the nave, and the cloisters and chapter-house, which, however, have disappeared; cloisters would come to be considered a necessity as soon as the secular canons were superseded by regulars. The early English clerestory of the nave seems to have been built in the time of the third prior, Peter, about the beginning of the thirteenth century. To the end of same century may be approximately assigned the vaulting of the nave aisles, the north porch, and a chapel attached to the north transept. Alterations of an extensive nature seem to have been begun in the fourteenth century; for to this date belong the rood screen, placed farther to the east than the old division between the ritual choir of the canons and the western part of the nave, which was probably given up to the lay dwellers in the parish,— and the splendid reredos. The Lady Chapel also was completed certainly before 1406, probably eleven years earlier. The fifteenth century saw the western tower built and the choir commenced and a great part of it finished, though the vaulting seems not to have been completed until the early part of the sixteenth century, as W. E. the initials of William Eyre, who was prior from 1502 to 1520, are to be seen on the bosses and the arch of the south choir aisle. Somewhat later still is the chantry at the east end of the south choir aisle, built by the last prior and dated 1529, and the chantry built by the last of the Plantagenets, Margaret, Countess of Salisbury, daughter of the Earl of Clarence and mother of Cardinal Pole, who at the age of seventy was executed by Henry VIII. in 1541.

Shortly before the dissolution in 1536 Prior Draper addressed a petition to Henry VIII. which is still in existence in the Record Office, praying that he would spare the Priory church, basing his request upon the desolate character of the district, the poverty of the house, and the fact that the church was not only a place for poor religious men, but also a parish church to the town and hamlets round about, whose inhabitants numbered from fifteen to sixteen hundred, that there was no place where any honest man on horseback or on foot might have succour or repose for the space of eight or nine miles, "but only this poor place of Christchurch, to which both rich and poor doth repair and repose." He goes on to say how it was of late years a place of secular canons, until the king's antecessors made it a place of canons regular, that "the poor, not only of the parish and town, but also of the country, were daily relieved and sustained with bread and ale, purposely baked and brewed for them weekly to no small quantities according to their foundation, and a house ordained purposely for them, and officers according duly given attendance to serve them to their great comfort and relief." But all the pleading was in vain. Commissioners were appointed, who presented their report to Lord Cromwell December 2, 1539. They say that "we found the Prior a very honest and conformable person, and the house well furnished with jewels and plate, whereof some be meet for the king's majesty's use." Then follows a list of the treasures of the abbey, of the yearly value of the several endowments, and of the officers of the Priory, thirteen in number besides the Prior. Prior Draper retired on a pension, and the site of the domestic buildings was conveyed to Stephen and Margaret Kirton. The domestic buildings themselves gradually disappeared, but the whole of the church was handed over to the parish as a church, the grant to the churchwardens being made by letters patent 23 October 32 Henry VIII. It conveyed to them "the choir body, bell-tower with seven bells, stones, timber, lead of roofing and gutters of the church and the cemetery on the north side." Since then the church has been served by vicars, the patronage being in the hands of the dean and chapter of Winchester until the present century, when the advowson was purchased by Lord Malmesbury.

During the present century much restoration has been done. The nave was vaulted in stucco in 1819 ; the west window was taken in hand in 1828 ; the pinnacles of the tower and the upper part of the turret containing the stairs were renewed in 1871 ; and constant repairs have been going on up to the present time ; and the principle that has guided the restorer has been, when any stonework has been removed to put in its place as exact a copy of the old as possible,—a principle that cannot be approved of, as it will lead, when the newness of the modern work has been toned down by time, to confusion between the genuine old work and the modern imitation of it. It is far better, when there is no question of stability but only of appearance, to leave the old stonework, even though much decayed, as it is, unscraped, untouched by the chisel, and where strength is needed to put in frankly nineteenth-century work, which could never by any possibility be mistaken for part of the original building.

One of the most glaring instances of injudicious restoration is to be met with in the apsidal chapel attached to the eastern side of the south transept. This work was carried out by the Hon. C. Harris, late Bishop of Gibraltar. The arcading is a nineteenth-century imitation of Norman work ; the pavement is glaringly modern. Of what interest, it may well be asked, is such work? Who would care to visit Christchurch to see it? The nineteenth-century carver cannot possibly produce work similar to that of the carver who lived in the twelfth century,— the conditions of his life are altogether different, his training bears no resemblance to that of the old artist, his work is a forgery, and a most clumsy one too. In this chapel we see this reprehensible practice carried to its fullest extent, but there are many other parts of the building which have suffered. Most of the arcading on the exterior of the transept is modern imita- tion, and the tracery of the windows of the south choir aisle has been entirely renewed ; no old stones, though many might have been used, have been reset in their original position. The arcading of the south aisle of the nave has been terribly tampered with. Possibly under the influence of time many of the shafts had partially crumbled, and the surface of the carved capitals had perished, so that the original design could not be made out ; but that was no reason for cutting away the ornamental work to make way for modern decoration which may or may not bear some slight resemblance to what was there before. Some of the piers of the nave arcading have also been partially renewed. By an act of much-to-be-con- demned vandalism the sub-arches of the two eastern bays of the south triforium of the nave were cut away to make room for faculty pews; recently a glaring white pillar has been introduced into the westernmost of these two bays, and two sub-arches built. If the same kind of work is carried out in the other, we shall see in all probability an attempt to copy the unique scale decoration which still exists on the tympanum under the corresponding principal arch on the north side, cut with modern tools with all the lifeless rigidity of modern work. Another mistake which has been made, is the scraping off of the plaster from the interior walls of the chamber known as St Michael's Loft, over the Lady Chapel, and the re-pointing of the stonework. Old builders invariably covered their rubble walls with plaster, but the modern restorer for some reason seems to hate plaster and prefers to show the coarse stonework which the builder never intended should be seen, and to emphasise the roughness by filling up the joints with conspicuous pointing. This, however, is not so destructive as much of the work which has been condemned above, because at any time the walls could be re-covered with a thin coat of smooth plaster laid on with a trowel, but not "floated,"—that is, not brought to a smooth surface by a long straightedge.

A large and old building such as this Priory Church will need almost constant repairs to keep it sound and safe, and the income from visitors' fees is quite sufficient for this purpose. It is, however, much to be feared that restoration and reconstruction will form far too large a part of the work done in this building. Every new ornamental stone, to make room for which some original stone is displaced, detracts from the value of the building from an archæological point of view; and though there may be some, or even many, who prefer the trim and smug appearance of modern work to that of the old, instinct with life, full of the thoughts of the builders and workers in wood and stone, whose bones have mouldered into dust in the garth of the vanished cloisters, and whose very names have in many cases been forgotten, yet we hope that those who have this priceless treasure in their keeping may recognise ere it is too late, that the result of a continuance of the process of restoration commenced about the middle of the nineteenth century will be the gradual conversion of a splendid memorial of bygone ages into a modern sham, and they themselves will be regarded, when true love of art becomes general, with the same indignation as that which they themselves feel with regard to those who pulled down the roof of the south transept and cut out the columns and sub-arches of the triforium in days before the Gothic revival set in. And the modern restorer has less excuse than the destroyer of a hundred years ago. If, like the vandals of the Georgian period, they had been blind to the beauties of architectural art, they would have had no sin, yet since they profess to see, therefore their sin will remain and their names will be held in perpetual reproach and everlasting contempt.

The foregoing historical sketch of the building has perforce been somewhat vague in dates, for, in the absence of documentary evidence, it is not easy to fix from architectural considerations alone the date of any particular piece of work within a limit of some twenty years or so. The out-of-the-way position of the Priory of Christchurch—for no great road ran through the town, and though it is near the sea there is no convenient harbour near it—has brought it to pass that it is scarcely mentioned in any mediæval chronicles. Its own fabric rolls and annals have been lost. Here and there, however, the date of a will or the inscription on a monument has enabled a more definite date to be arrived at. The dates also of the dedications of some of the many altars are known— viz. that of the Holy Saviour, used by the canons as their high altar, and that of St Stephen, dedicated by the Bishop of Ross in 1199; that of the altar of the Holy Trinity, which stood in the nave, and was the high altar of the parish ; and those of the altars of SS. Peter and Paul, SS. Augustine and Gregory and all the Prophets, dedicated by Walter, Bishop of Whitherne, on November 7, 1214 ; that of the altar of St John the Baptist and St Edmund, dedicated on December 7, 1214, by the same bishop; and that of the altar of SS. Michael and Martin, dedicated by the Bishop of the Isles in 1221.

CHAPTER II

THE EXTERIOR

THE exterior of the church of Christchurch Priory may be well seen from several points of view. The churchyard lies to the north of the building, extending beyond it both to the east and west. On the south side, where all the domestic buildings of the Priory once stood, there is a modern house and private grounds. All that belongs to the church is a path running under the walls as far as the east corner of the transept, where a garden door stops farther progress. Several glimpses of the building, however, may be obtained on the way down to the Stour, and seen from the south side of this river, the church rises above its surroundings, and forms a conspicuous object. A good general view on the north-east may also be obtained from a bridge over the Avon. From this point of view the great length of the church is apparent; on the right-hand side may be seen the ruins of the Norman keep of the castle on its artificial mound, and nearer to the bridge the remains of a twelfth-century Norman house. From the churchyard, also, the whole north side of the church may be seen at once, and many striking features will be noticed. Among these, the circular staircase attached to the transept, with its rich diaper work; Norman arcading of interlacing arches running round the transept; the large windows of the choir clerestory, so wide and closely set together that the whole wall seems as though composed of glass—through which, and the windows of the opposite wall, the light of the sky can be seen; and lastly, the upper storey of the Lady Chapel with its row of windows of a domestic type.

A systematic examination of the exterior may best be begun with the **Western Tower**. This is of fifteenth-century date, and is set partially within the church—that is to say, its builder did not add it to the west of the church, making an archway

through the previously existing west front, but pulled down the whole west wall of the nave, leaving, however, the west walls of the aisles, and carried the north and south walls of the new tower as far back into the church as the space occupied by the western bay, thus leaving two spaces at the west end of the aisles, one now used as a vestry, the other as

TOWER DOOR.

a kind of lumber-room. In the west face of the tower is a doorway under a rectangular label; in the spandrels are two shields, bearing the arms of the Priory, and of the Montacutes and Monthermers, Earls of Salisbury. The doors are modern. Immediately above the doorway is a large window with three tiers, each containing six lights. The head of the window above these is of an ordinary Perpendicular character. The tracery was restored in 1828. Above this window is a niche containing a figure of Christ. The upper stage, which contains the bells, has two two-light windows in each face, each light being divided by a transom. These windows are not glazed, but are furnished with louvre-boards. The tower is crowned with a pierced battlemented parapet having pinnacles at the corners and at the middles of each side; within this rises

NORTH PORCH.

a low pyramidal roof. The stair turret runs up at the north-east angle of the tower; this is octagonal, and is crowned with a parapet and crocketed pinnacles; the upper part of this turret and the pinnacles were renewed in 1871. The tower is strengthened by two buttresses at right angles to each other at each of the two western angles. On either side of the tower, as already explained, may be seen the west end of the nave aisles; these have windows with Perpendicular tracery, and on the north wall of the north aisle is a plain, round-headed doorway cut through the wall in modern time, with a Perpendicular window over it.

Next comes the **North Porch,** with a chamber above it—here, as in many other churches, the chief entrance into the building. Its great dimensions, both in length and height, however, are remarkable; it projects 40 feet beyond the aisle wall, and its own side walls rise nearly to the height of the clerestory of the church. Its south end does not extend beyond the wall of the aisle, so that there is a space between the upper part of the porch and the clerestory. The upper part above the porch proper contains, as mentioned above, a lofty chamber, probably originally the muniment-room. This is lighted by two pairs of narrow single-light windows on either side, and by a similar pair in the north face beneath the obtuse-angled gable. This room is, no doubt, a later addition. The entrance into the porch is a beautiful, deeply-recessed archway of thirteenth-century date, with numerous shafts of Purbeck marble on either side. Within the porch the side walls are divided into two compartments, each of which is composed of two pointed arches beneath another larger pointed arch, with a cinquefoil in the head. On the west side, near the outer archway, is a cinquefoiled recess, with shafts of Purbeck marble and foliated cusps. This is said originally to have contained a desk, at which the prior met the parishioners and signed deeds. A stone seat runs along each side of the porch walls. The double doorway which leads into the church is very beautiful and rich Early English work. From six Purbeck marble shafts on either side spring the orders of the enclosing archway; the heads of the double doorways themselves are cinquefoiled arches with foliated cusps. At the jambs, and dividing the two doors, are clusters of Purbeck marble shafts, with moulded capitals. In the tympanum is a quatrefoil, the upper part of which projects so as to form a canopy. This was, no doubt, intended to contain some carved subject, possibly the Doom. Very extensive restoration was carried out in the groining and porch generally, in 1862.

The wall of the **North Aisle** between the porch and the transept is divided into six compartments by Early English buttresses with gabled heads. This wall was built in Norman times, as may be seen from the small round-headed windows which light the clerestory, but was in Early English times faced with fresh ashlar, which conceals the

THE NORTH DOOR.

F

Norman arcading of intersecting arches which ran along this wall. The triforium windows on this side are not, though they are on the south side, regularly arranged; there are none in the two western divisions, while between the easternmost buttress and the transept there are two. Six late thirteenth-century windows were cut through this wall — these are all of similar design; they consist of two lights under a comprising arch, with a circle in the head. The clerestory windows are of plainer character. Each window consists of two simple lancets set under a recessed arch without any hood moulding; the tympana also above the lancet heads are not pierced or decorated in any way; in fact, the whole clerestory is remarkably plain. Between the windows are flat buttresses. The aisles are covered with lean-to roofs of lead, the nave itself with a tiled roof of medium pitch. The gable at the east end of the nave, and indications on the east face of the tower, show that the pitch of the roof was once higher, and that it must have been lowered at some time after the tower was built in the fifteenth century.

The **North Transept** is most interesting. Its west wall contains two round-headed windows with billet moulding, the northern one blocked up; and at the north-west corner is a cluster of cylindrical shafts running up to about the same height as the walls of the aisle. Why they terminated here it is hard to say; they may mark the termination of the original Norman wall. This wall may not have risen above this height, or the upper part may have been taken down and rebuilt when the large Perpendicular window was inserted in the north end of the transept. At the north-east corner of the transept stands a richly-ornamented turret of Norman date. Round the lower part of this the arcade of intersecting arches which runs round the whole transept is carried; above this, round the turret, runs an arcading of semicircular-headed arches springing from pairs of shafts; above this the wall is decorated with diaper work.; and finally, another arcading, this time of round-headed arches rising from single shafts, encircles the turret. The turret is capped by a sloping roof of stone attached to the transept wall. This turret is worthy of close attention, because it shows how the Norman builders hated monotony; each stage has its own decoration unlike that of any other; and, moreover, there are variations in the shafts of the arcading—some are plain, some decorated in one way, some

THE NORTH TRANSEPT IN 1810.
(From Britton's "Architectural Antiquities.")

in another. The same love of variety may be seen here that
lends so great a charm on a larger scale to Flambard's glorious

nave at Durham. No doubt this north transept had attached to its east wall an apsidal Norman chapel similar to that which still exists on the eastern side of the south transept, but this had to make way for an addition of two chapels, which we may assign, from the character of their architecture, to the latter end of the thirteenth century. The northern chapel is lighted by a three-light window with three foliated circles in the head, which is rather sharp pointed, and the southern one by a two-light window with one foliated arch. These are beautiful examples of plate tracery. Above these chapels is a small chamber lighted by a window of similar character. This is supposed to have been the tracing room, where the various architectural designs for the building were drawn.

To the east of the transept may be seen the **Choir** and **Presbytery,** with its four clerestory windows; the **Choir Aisle,** also with four windows; the **Lady Chapel**, with the octagonal turret-staircase leading into Saint Michael's Loft above it. It will be noticed that there is no window in the aisle under the western clerestory window of the choir, as the space where this would have been found is occupied by the two chapels to the east of the transept, and also that the aisle extends beyond the choir and flanks the western part of the Lady Chapel. The whole of this part of the church is of Perpendicular character. The windows of the choir aisles are low, the arches are depressed, and the curvature of each side of the arch is so slight that they appear almost straight lines. The body of these windows contains four lights; in the head, each of these is subdivided into two. Between the aisle windows are buttresses, which, with the exception of the one opposite the east wall of the choir, which terminates in a gable, have pinnacled cappings; and from each of these, save the gabled one, a flying buttress is carried over the roof of the aisle and rests against the choir wall. The aisle roof is flat, and at the top of the outer wall runs a plain parapet pierced with quatrefoil openings. The clerestory windows are of great size and are set close together. The choir roof is flat and is quite invisible from the exterior. There can be little doubt that a parapet at one time ran along the tops of the clerestory walls, but this has disappeared. The Lady Chapel has on either side three large Perpendicular windows; the arches of these as well as those of the clerestory have pointed heads. The western half of the central window of the Lady Chapel is blocked up by the later-built octagonal

THE NORTH TRANSEPT.

turret containing the staircase to Saint Michael's Loft. The staircase commences in an octagonal turret at the north-east corner of the choir aisle, - this rises above the aisle roof, the stairs are then carried above the east wall of the choir aisle and then into the octagonal turret, which runs up the wall of the Lady Chapel and the loft above, and rises to some height above the parapet. There is a similar staircase on the south side, but the turret does not rise quite so high above the roof. There are five square-headed two-light windows on either side of St Michael's Loft, the lights being divided by transoms, the upper parts foliated. At the east end is a three-light window without any transom, with an obtuse arch under a dripstone. The loft has a parapet all round it pierced with quatrefoil openings. Some of this parapet, at any rate, is modern, as, in a photograph of the north side taken in 1884, the parapet is only shown to the east of the turret. As restoration work is constantly going on at the church, the money paid by visitors for viewing the interior (sixpence a head, which produces over £500 a year) being devoted to this object, the parapet will doubtless in course of time be extended along the walls of the choir, and will certainly add to the beauty of the church; and as nothing will be destroyed to make room for it, such an addition will not be open to the same objection as much of the work done by restoration committees.

The buttresses at the east angles of the Lady Chapel are set diagonally, and rise in five stages; the upper stage of each is square, in section, with the faces parallel to the walls of the church, and reaches a higher level than the parapet, and is finished with a flat cap. The large east window is a Perpendicular one of five lights. From the base of the south-east buttress runs a wall dividing the burying-ground from the gardens of the house, to the south of the church, which stands on the site of the domestic buildings of the priory. The portion of the wall of the Lady Chapel beneath the easternmost window on the north side is modern. Here Mr Ferrey, the architect, by whom much of the restoration was carried out, discovered traces of an external chantry and the marks of an arcading corresponding to that still remaining on the inside.

The object of the chamber above the Lady Chapel is uncertain,—in 1617 it is described as "St Michael's Loft," in 1666 the parishioners described it as "heretofore a chapter-house," when petitioning the bishop to allow it to be used as a school. But if it was ever used as a chapter-house, it could only have been for a short time, as there is evidence that there was a chapter-house to the south side of the choir in the twelfth century, and that this remained as late as 1498. The south

THE SOUTH AISLE OF NAVE.

side of the Lady Chapel and choir correspond very closely with the north side, but there are several differences to be noticed between the south and north transepts. On the eastern side of the **South Transept** the Norman apsidal chapel still remains. This has a semi-conical roof with chevron table moulding under it, and two windows—one of original Norman work, the other a three-light Early English window. A sacristy of Early English date stands to the east of the apsidal chapel, and occupies the space between the apse and the south choir wall. At the south-east corner of the transept there is a circular stair turret corresponding to some extent with the turret at the north-east angle of the north transept; this, in the second stage, becomes octagonal in section, and rises above the parapet of the transept. In the south face is a depressed segmental window, much smaller than the corresponding window on the north side, under a gabled parapet. The pitch of the roof of the south transept is much higher than that of the north transept, and the upper part of the transept does not abut against the walls of the church. Two tiers of corbel brackets on the south wall, and traces of two Norman windows seem to indicate that here, as elsewhere, a slype, with a room above it, intervened between the south end of the transept and the chapter-house. This slype was generally a passage connecting the cloister garth with the smaller garth to the south of the choir which was often used as a burying-place for the abbots or priors, as the case may be, and was the place where the monks or canons interviewed visitors and chapmen. The room above was often used as the library. The south of the **Nave** is decidedly inferior in interest to the north. The cloisters have entirely disappeared, but a series of round-headed arches, formed of stucco, may conceal a stone arcading similar to that hidden by the Early English facing of the north wall. The small round-headed windows giving light to the triforium are more regularly arranged than on the north side; there is one, and only one, in each division between the buttresses. There were, as usual, two doors in this wall: one for the canons, in the wall opposite to the west of the cloister, one close to the transept for the prior; both are now blocked up. The prior's door, in the injunction of Langton, 1498, is directed to be kept locked, save when on festivals a procession passed through it. This doorway is of early thirteenth-century work; it is round-headed, and is French in character. There is a legend that a party of French monks, terrified by a dragon which rose out of the sea, possibly an ancestor of the sea-serpent of more modern days, put in to Christchurch haven, and were entertained by the canons, with whom they abode for many years; possibly this door may be of their workmanship or design. In the south wall a large aumbry or cupboard, in the thickness of the walls, may be seen; in this possibly the canons kept the books that they had brought from the library for study. What the windows in this aisle were we cannot say—originally, no doubt, Norman, for the westernmost window is still of this style; but the others, which were widened either in Early English or Decorated times, are now all filled with nineteenth-century tracery of Decorated type. The buttresses between the windows, unlike those on the north side, are flat Norman ones. Towards the west end of the aisle a passage has in modern times been cut through the wall, and when this was done remains of a staircase which, no doubt, led to the dormitory, were discovered. The clerestory, on this side, is of the same plain character as on the north side.

In a line with the south wall, but some little distance to the west, still stands a house which was once the porter's lodge, close to the site of the gatehouse. The porter's lodge was built by Prior Draper II. in the sixteenth century. The remains of the domestic buildings are very scanty—some old walls near the modern mill, occupying, no doubt, the site of the mill where the canons' corn was ground; some vestiges of the fish ponds; some few traces of walls and foundations, are all that have come down to modern days. From the similarity of arrangement in the buildings of religious houses, however, we can, with great certainty, assign the sites for the various parts—the dormitory over the cellarage, to the west of the cloister garth; the refectory to south of it; the calefactory, chapter-house, slype, to the east; and the prior's lodgings to the south of the choir, forming the lesser garth; the barns, bakery, and brew-house to the south-west of the church, near the porter's lodge and gatehouse. The prior had a country house at Heron Court, a grange at Somerford, and another at St Austin's, near Lymington. It must be understood that the choir was the church of the canons, and, as was common in churches served by Augustinian canons, the nave was used for the services which the laity of the district attended.

It is noteworthy that whether owing to the purity of the air, so different from that which exists in the large cities where so many of the cathedral churches stand, or from the goodness of the stone, most of the Priory Church is in most excellent preservation. Carving which, we are assured, has never been retouched with a chisel since it was first cut, remains as sharp and clearly cut as though it were the work of the nineteenth century; possibly some of its excellence is due to the preservative effect of the whitewash with which it was once covered, and which has been cleaned off with water and a stiff bristled brush.

The stone of which the north side of the nave is built came from Binstead; the limestone columns from Henden Hill; the Norman round turret and the choir is built of Portland stone; while Purbeck marble shafts are used in the north porch, and of the fine white stone from Caen in Normandy, the Salisbury and Draper chantries in the interior are constructed. These, though now about four hundred years old, are absolutely sharp in all the carving. There is a tombstone to the north of the porch which bears a curious inscription as follows :—" We were not slayne but raysd, raysd not to life but to be byried twice by men of strife. What rest could the living have when dead had none agree amongst you heere we ten are one. Hen. Rogers died Aprill 17 1641." This inscription has been variously explained. It is said by some that Cromwell, afterwards Protector, was at Christchurch, and dug up some lead coffins to make bullets for his soldiers, and flung the bodies out of ten such coffins into one grave; but this is manifestly incorrect. Oliver Cromwell was never at Christchurch, though Thomas Cromwell probably was, and here, as elsewhere, the two have been confounded. In many cases poor Oliver has had to bear the blame for destruction caused to churches by his less well-known namesake, the great destroyer of religious houses in the days of the eighth Henry. But neither of them had anything to do with this tomb, nor were the Parliamentary forces guilty of tampering with the coffins of the dead in the parish burying-ground at Christchurch. The very date precludes the idea, for the civil war did not begin till more than fifteen months after the date

carved on this stone ; and we may give the Roundheads credit
for more sense than to be digging up coffins to make their
bullets with, when there was abundance of lead to be had
for the stripping on the roof of the Priory Church. A far more
probable explanation is that which states that the ten bodies
here interred were those of ten shipwrecked sailors, who were
first buried on the cliffs near the spot where they were washed
ashore ; but the lord of the manor, when he heard thereof,
waxed exceeding wroth, and a strife ensued between him
and one Henry Rogers, Mayor of Christchurch, the former
insisting on their removal to consecrated ground, the latter
objecting to the removal, probably on the ground of expense ;
but in the end the lord of the manor had his way. But the
mayor, to save the cost of ten separate graves, had them
all buried in one, and placed this inscription over their
remains as a protest against the conduct of the lord of the
manor in moving their remains from their first resting-
place.

The graveyard at the present time is neatly kept and well
cared for. The headstones have not, as they have been in
many other places, tampered with ; and though many of the
alterations made in the restoration will not gain the approval
of archæologists, yet some have been judiciously done, and
some that are in contemplation will certainly have the result
of rendering once more visible beautiful mediæval work, long
concealed by ugly modern additions.

CHAPTER III

A RAPID walk round the interior of the Priory Church shows that it practically consists of three main portions, almost entirely divided from each other—the **Nave,** the **Choir,** and the **Lady Chapel.** The solid rood screen, pierced by one narrow doorway, forms an effectual division between the nave and choir, while the stone reredos and the wall above it, running right up to the vaulting, entirely separates the latter from the Lady Chapel. In mediæval times the choir was reserved for the use of the canons; the nave was the parish church with its own high altar; the rood loft was an excellent point of vantage from which a preacher could address a large congregation. In those times pews had not been introduced; open benches may have existed. At present the nave is occupied by pews; these with their cast-iron poppies were erected in 1840, and were then higher than at present. Still, even in their present form, they hide the bases of the pillars, and might with much advantage be swept away, and their places taken by open benches or movable chairs. The pews in the transepts are of older date; these, together with the galleries above them—that in the south transept supporting the organ—are a sad disfigurement to the church, and it is to be hoped that they will be soon removed; they hide some splendid Norman work. The case of the north gallery is worse than the south, as a staircase leading to it disfigures the beautiful Early English chapel attached to the east side of the transept. This gallery, however, contains some faculty pews. All the owners of these, save one, consented to its removal; but one stood out against it, and, having the legal right to prevent any alteration, has up to the present time kept the gallery intact. But as he has recently died there can be little doubt that no long time will now elapse before this disfigurement to the church will be a thing of the past. There seems little need for the gallery, as there is ample accommodation on the floor of the church for any congregation that is likely to assemble within the walls. Many alterations, some of which are certainly improvements, have already been made. In an engraving, dated 1834, the organ is represented standing on the rood screen, probably the best place for it; and the four eastern bays of the nave are seen to be partitioned off by a wooden screen with a rod for curtains. On a level with the capitals of the pillars, to the west of this partition, stands the font. At this time also the triforium was boarded off in order to shut out draughts and cold; but this boarding has happily been swept away, the partition across the nave has been removed, and an oaken screen with glazed panels runs across the church, cutting off the western bay from

THE NAVE IN 1834.

the remainder of the nave. The font, a modern one, now stands under the tower; a modern pulpit on the south side, under the crossing, where also desks for the clergy and choir have been placed. It is now the custom on Sunday mornings to read the whole of the service up to the end of the Nicene Creed, in the nave; after the sermon is over, the communicants alone enter the choir to receive the sacrament.

The choir is also used for week-day services. The Lady Chapel is not used. The nave is Early Norman work, and was chiefly built during the reign of William II.; the clerestory, however, was added at the beginning of the thirteenth century by Peter, who was prior from 1195 to 1225. The original nave was probably covered by a flat wooden ceiling, the Early Norman builders rarely venturing to span any wide space by a stone vaulting. The present vaulting is of stucco, and was added by Garbett in 1819. The roof was altered in Perpendicular times more than once, as indications of a higher pitched roof than the present one exists on the east face of the fifteenth-century tower. As springing stones for a vaulted roof exist, it is probable that a stone roof was at one time contemplated; but possibly the idea was abandoned on account of the fear that the walls, unsupported by any exterior flying buttress to resist the thrust, would not have borne the weight. It will be remembered that such buttresses are to be met with along the walls of the choir, which is covered with a stone vaulting. The nave consists of seven bays. The pillars of this arcading, unlike those of Flambard's nave at Durham, are not cylindrical, but consist of half columns set against piers rectangular in section. The capitals are of the early cushion shape; some of them seem to have been subsequently carved with ornamentation which bears some resemblance to classical forms. The wall spaces above the semicircular arches, and below the chevron string-course which runs beneath the triforium, are decorated with hatchet-work carving, as will be seen from the illustrations. The triforium on either side consists, in each bay, of two coupled arches supported by a central pillar, enclosed by a comprising arch with bold mouldings and double columns, separated by square members. The most beautiful bay is the easternmost, on the north side, where the wall surface above the smaller arches, and beneath the enclosing arch, is carved with a kind of scale-work. Possibly the opposite bay, on the south side, was as richly ornamented, but the lower arches and the central column no longer exist, as they were cut away to make room for a faculty pew in 1820. These two bays were included within the original Norman choir. The central shaft, on the north side, is twisted. Two of the central shafts, on the south side, are richly ornamented

THE NAVE.

—one with twisted decoration, the other with a projecting
reticulated pattern. The shaft and sub-arches of the second

NORTH ARCADE OF NAVE.

bay from the east on this side is a modern renewal, as
here also the old work was destroyed in 1820 to make room

FROM THE NORTH TRIFORIUM.

G

for a pew. The north triforium can be reached by a staircase
continued up into the tower, entered from the western part
of the aisle; access to the south triforium can only be
gained by the use of a ladder. The north triforium deserves
examination. It will be found that pointed arches have been added at the back, and buttresses have been built against the back of the wall behind the arches; the floor is rendered uneven by humps necessitated by the Early English vault-ing of the aisle below—probably the aisles were originally covered with a barrel roof. At the east end of the north triforium an arch may be seen, which once opened out into the transept; this is now walled up, and traces of painting may still be seen on it. There is a pass-age under the clerestory, to which access may be obtained by a passage across the transept; this was, no doubt, made in order that the shutters of the windows might be opened or closed, according to the state of the weather. From the staircase which leads up to the north triforium a passage leads into the chamber over the north porch. This is a large room, about 40 feet in length from north to south, and is now used as a practising room for the choir; it is fitted with benches and a grand piano, and has a modern wooden gallery running along its south end.

BAY OF THE TRIFORIUM, SOUTH SIDE.

The **South Aisle** is much more elaborately decorated than
the north. Along the south wall runs a fine Norman arcade,
the arches ornamented with billet and cable moulding. The
window in the western bay is the original Norman one;
the others were altered either in Early English or Decorated

THE SOUTH AISLE OF NAVE.

times, and are now filled with modern tracery in the Decorated
style designed by Mr Ferrey. In the third bay is a holy water
stoop, and in the fifth a large aumbry or recess, entered by
a door; in this used to be kept the bier and lights used at
funerals. Along the walls of each aisle runs a stone bench.
There is no arcading on the wall of the north aisle. The
vaulting of both aisles is Early English, dating from the time
of Peter, the third prior, who, as previously stated, built
the clerestory. The tracery of the north aisle windows
is transitional in character between Early English and
Decorated.

The **Transepts** are much encumbered by modern pews and
galleries, and it is only by careful examination that much of
the beautiful work that they contain can be seen. The arch
opening from the south aisle into the transept is Early English,
and the skilful junction of Early English and Norman work
at this point is deserving of attention. This transept was at
one time covered by a stone vaulting, which was destroyed at
the latter end of the eighteenth century and in the beginning
of the nineteenth. Some of the bosses taken from this may
be seen, piled up with the old font and other fragments, at
the west end of the north choir aisle. The west wall of the
transept contains a Norman window. A doorway into the
slype remains in the wall, and communicates with a wall
passage. At the eastern side of the transept an arch opens
out into an apsidal chapel, but pews block up the entrance.
This chapel has been so completly restored that it has a
thoroughly neat and modern appearance, and has lost all
its archæological value; round it runs a Norman arcade, and
on the north side an aumbry may be seen. The north
transept retains its Norman arcading, which, fortunately, has
not been touched by the restorer's hand; how long it may
escape is doubtful, as it is much mutilated. Still, as it is simply
decorative, and not necessary for the stability of the wall,
it would be well to leave it untouched, as genuine old work,
even though it may have suffered at the hand of time or of
former generations, is, from a decorative point of view, in-
finitely preferable to any modern reproduction. There are
two small windows in the west wall to light the wall passage
to the clerestory, which is reached by a gallery running across
the base of the north window. In the north wall, behind the

THE MONTACUTE CHANTRY.

back of the pews, is a thirteenth-century recess. From this transept access is gained to the circular staircase leading downward to the crypt and upward to the small chamber above the eastern chapels. This is popularly known as Oliver Cromwell's harness room, and marks are shown on the wall supposed to have been holes for the insertion of pegs whereon he hung his harness; but as the Protector never came to Christchurch, all this is purely mythical. On one of the walls Mr Ferrey, the architect, found a design for a window; this he copied, and used when designing the tracery of the window he inserted over the prior's door at the east end of the south aisle of the nave. This tracing chamber is lighted by a two-light window with a quatrefoil in the head in the eastern wall. The two chapels below are beautiful examples of transition work from the Early English to the Decorated style; they were built by the De Redvers, Earls of Devon, the last of whom died in 1263. The eagles of the Montacute and Monthermer families appear in this chantry. There are two windows in the eastern wall. The larger, on the north, consists of three lights, with three circles in the head; the foliation of these outside the glass forms cinquefoil openings; the smaller window is of a similar character, but consists of two lights only, with a single foliated arch above them. An archway, widely splayed, on the western side, opens into the transept, and another archway opens into the choir aisle; this has a panelled pier, standing a little apart from the eastern side, designed to support the arch, which probably was found to be giving way. The shafts along the eastern wall, the capitals of one of which is carved with a number of heads said to represent the twelve apostles, should be noticed; the vaulting ribs are also interesting, especially the joggled ribs seen over the window. A stone altar stood in one of these chantries until 1780. These chapels are sadly disfigured by a mean staircase which leads into the transept gallery; it is devoutly to be hoped that before long this may be removed, and the exquisite beauty of the chapels seen without any inharmonious and irritating feature such as this staircase undoubtedly is. Below the transept is an Early Norman crypt; it is thought by some, from the rudeness of the work, that it may be of earlier date than the existing church, and that it belonged to the original church which Flambard

THE NORTH AISLE OF NAVE.

destroyed to make room for his more splendid edifice. In it were discovered a number of human bones, which were re-interred in the churchyard. It has a plain barrel roof, divided by broad flat arches rising from pilasters.

It has often been debated whether or not the church ever possessed a central tower. There is no documentary evidence bearing on the question. It may be said that if a tower existed and fell, or was pulled down for any reason, some record would have remained; but the records connected with the building are fragmentary, and it by no means follows that the absence of record proves the non-existence of such a tower. In the case of Wimborne Minster the church-warden's accounts contain no record of the building or of the fall of the spire, yet we know from outside testimony that such a spire did fall in 1600, and that a representation of it occurs on a seal. So here at Christchurch a seal is in ex-istence on which the church is represented with a central tower of two storeys, the lower plain, the upper lighted by two round-headed windows and capped by a low pyramidal spire or roof with a tall cross on the summit. This is exactly what one would expect to find: a central tower is almost always found in Norman churches, especially collegiate churches; and the pyramidal roof was almost certainly the usual form in which these early towers were finished. The battlemented parapets which we so often meet with in Norman towers are in all cases more recent additions. Moreover, the massive arches and piers at the corners indicate that a tower was contemplated, even if it were never built. In the east gable of the nave as it at present exists, two round-headed windows may be seen. It is highly probable that this gable once formed part of the east wall of the tower, and when the tower was removed this wall was converted into a gable. Everything to the east of the crossing being of late fourteenth or early fifteenth century date, indicates that extensive alterations were made at that time; and if a tower and spire had previously existed, it must have been removed before this date. In the centre of the carving over the doorway leading into the Draper chantry, dated 1529, there is a representation of a church with a central tower and spire. Of course, no such steeple existed at the time this chantry was built, but it may have been a copy of some then existing representation of the building as it had appeared in former times. There are also two other carvings of angels carrying a model of a church with a central tower—one near the Salisbury chantry, one on the choir roof.

The nave is divided from the choir by a splendid rood screen 16 feet 6 inches high, 33 feet long, and 9 feet thick. The western face of this projects beyond the line join-

THE CRYPT.

ing the east walls of the two transepts; its eastern face rests against the eastern piers intended to support the central tower. It was extensively restored by Mr Ferrey in 1848, who considered that it may have been removed from some conventual church after the dissolution of the monasteries in the time of Henry VIII. and re-erected here. But there does not seem to be any real grounds for supposing that it was not expressly built for this church. Its character indicates a date somewhat late in the fourteenth century. In the centre is a narrow doorway and a passage

into the choir; from the north side of this passage a flight
of steps leads to the top of the loft. The base of the screen
is plain; above this is a row of thirteen panelled quatrefoils
on each side of the doorway—each containing a plain shield,
over these a string course, then two rows of canopied niches,
the upper row consisting of twelve, the lower, owing to the
doorway occupying the central space, of only ten. The
lower niches have pedestals, each formed of four short
columns with detached bases but with large capitals, which
meet one another above; these capitals are richly carved
with foliage. No doubt, on the level space thus formed
statues at one time stood. Woodwork screens with glazed
doors and panels, made from an oak screen which formerly
was placed across the south transept, run across the western
ends of the choir aisles, so that when the doors of these and
of the rood screen are locked, the eastern arm of the cross is
entirely shut off from the rest of the church.

The **Choir** is entirely Perpendicular in character, and it
seems to have been begun in the time of Henry VI. but
not to have been completed until the time of Henry VII.,
and some of the carving of the stalls is of still later date.
Leland says of it, "Baldwin, Earl of Devon, was the first
founder, and his successors to the time of Isabella de
Fortibus,* and at present the Earls of Salisbury are regarded as founders." Four large clerestory windows on
either side light the choir. The wall beneath these is
continued downwards to the floor, but under each window
a low obtusely-pointed depressed archway is cut leading into
the aisles. Between the bottom of each clerestory window
and the heads of these arches the wall is panelled as with
window mullions and tracery, so that the appearance from
the inner side may be best understood by imagining that
each window extended from floor to roof, but that the upper
part alone is glazed, the lower cut away for the arch leading into the aisle, and the lower lights beneath the transom
blocked up with masonry. These lower arches are more
or less blocked up. The Salisbury chapel blocks up the
north-eastern one completely; the sedilia, no doubt, occupied
the opposite one, where now a modern altar tomb may be

---

* She lived in the latter half of the thirteenth century.

THE ROOD SCREEN.

seen. The next on each side to the west is open, and flights of steps under them lead down to the aisles; the woodwork at the back of the choir stalls close the remaining two on the inside, and on the outside chantry chapels, opening one into the north one into the south aisle, stand under the second arch on each side counting from the rood screen. The upper stalls number in all thirty-six, fifteen on either side, and six with their backs to the rood screen. There is, also, a lower range of stalls on the north and south. The prior's and sub-prior's stalls on either side the doorway in the screen looking east are canopied, as also is the precentor's at the east end of the south side. The arms of the stalls are quaintly carved with various grotesque figures, as are also the misereres; the upper parts of the panels behind the upper stalls are also carved in low relief; above these is a projecting cornice decorated with pinnacles. The stalls are late Perpendicular work, the wainscoting behind the stalls being later still, as we can see from the subjects carved on the upper part of each panel. Some of the misereres are, however, very old — one dates back to about 1200, another to 1300, others are of later date, and most of them belong to the same period as the stalls. The older ones were found lying about in the lumber of the church, and have been placed in recent years in some of the stalls the seats of which had been lost or stolen. The older seats may have belonged to the original Norman choir. As the term "miserere" may not be understood by all our readers, it may be well to quote from Parker's "Glossary of Architecture" the following description:— "Miserere, Misericorde, Patience, or Pretella, is the projecting bracket on the under-side of the seats of stalls in churches:

STALL SEAT.
(Date about 1200.)
South Side.

STALL SEAT.
North Side.

STALL SEAT.
North Side.

CHOIR STALLS

these, where perfect, are fixed with hinges so that they may be turned up, and when this is done the projection of the miserere is sufficient, without actually forming a seat, to afford very considerable rest to any one leaning upon it. They were allowed as a relief to the infirm during the long services that were required to be performed by ecclesiastics in a standing

MISERERE ON STALL SEAT. (*Circa* 1300.)

posture. They are always more or less ornamented with carvings of leaves, small figures, animals, etc., which are generally very boldly cut. Examples are to be found in almost all ancient churches which retain any of the ancient stalls—one of the oldest remaining specimens is in Henry VII.'s Chapel at Westminster; it is in the style of the thirteenth century." When Parker wrote the last sentence the still older miserere now to be seen at Christchurch had not been discovered—this is the earliest known specimen.

It is curious to notice the absence of reverence on the part of the mediæval canons, according to our modern notions, that

THE CHOIR.

these quaint carvings indicate. One might have expected that inside the church the subjects would have always been of a sacred nature, rude perhaps, and grotesque from their rudeness. Such carvings are found in many places, but here at Christchurch we have satirical subjects, caricatures of contemporaries, some indeed of so objectionable a character that they have been removed of late years. A few examples of these carvings will be given. On the arm of one of the stalls a fox is represented preaching to a flock of geese, a cock acting as clerk. On one of the misereres we have a pair of devils somewhat resembling monkeys tempting an angel, a goose bringing an offering on a plate to a quaint figure, a man with a hatchet employed in carving, a man with a hole in the back of his garments fastened with a pin, besides various animals, fishes, mermaids, and monsters. On the wainscoting we have the heads of Henry VII., Henry VIII., Catharine of Aragon, Anne Boleyn, Cardinal Campeggio, the King of Scots, and the Duchess of Burgundy, who assisted Perkin Warbeck in his attempt to gain the crown of England, and two canons disputing over a cup, which is placed between their faces. This last carving probably has some reference to the granting of the cup to the laity in time of Henry VIII.

The vaulting of the choir is of a somewhat unusual character : the pendants are especially worthy of notice. It is difficult to describe the manner in which they are placed, but the illustration shows their character and position. The short connecting ribs of the vaulting form a stellated cross over the presbytery. Some colour may still be seen on the carved work of this portion of the church, and the initials of William Eyre, prior 1502-1520, appear on the bosses.

The east wall of the presbytery contains no window, but is occupied by a beautiful stone reredos carved with a representation of the tree of Jesse. It is divided into three tiers with five compartments in each, the central one wider than the two on either side; the space above it and beneath the vaulting is occupied by a wall, in which a doorway now blocked up may be seen. The outer compartments of the lowest tier contain doors leading to a platform behind the reredos ; between them stands an oak altar, the gift of A. N. Welby Pugin in 1831. Above the altar in the central compartment Jesse lies asleep, on the left hand David plays upon his harp, on the right sits

THE REREDOS.

H

Solomon deeply meditating. Above Jesse we have in one
carving an amalgamated representation of the birth of Christ
and the visit of the Wise Men. On the left hand sits the Virgin
Mary with her Child, fully clothed in a long garment, not
wrapped in swaddling clothes, standing in her lap; behind her
stands a man, probably Joseph; and before her kneels one of
the Wise Men offering his gift of gold in the form of a plain
tankard; on the right behind him stand his two fellows, one
carrying a pot of myrrh, the other a boat-shaped vessel, probably intended for a censer containing frankincense. On a
bracket above the head of the kneeling Wise Man, the
shepherds kneel in adoration; nor are the flocks that they
were tending forgotten, for several sheep may be seen on a
hill-top above their heads. Thirty-two small figures may be
counted in niches in the buttresses dividing the compartments;
crockets, finials, and pinnacles decorate the various canopies
over the carvings. This reredos is apparently of late Decorated date, and therefore earlier than the fifteenth-century choir.
Possibly it was an addition to the Norman choir before this
was removed to make room for the existing one. Mr Ferrey
was of opinion that it may have once stood across the nave
between the second piers from the east, thus forming a
reredos for the western part of the nave, which was used
as the church of the parish. Below the presbytery is a
Norman crypt, now converted into a vault for the Malmesbury family. It has already been mentioned that there
are doors on either side of the altar, leading to a kind of
gallery or platform behind the reredos; these were designed to
allow certain ceremonial compassings of the altar, and it is
possible that steps led down from the platform to the ambulatory. On the east side of these doorways there are corbel
heads under the arches, and the walls of the platform are
panelled. Within the altar rails is a slab bearing the name of
Baldwin IV., the seventh Earl of Devon. On the south side
is the monument of Lady Fitzharris, who died in 1815; it is a
statue by Flaxman representing the Lady teaching her two sons
from the Bible. Farther to the east is the altar tomb of the
Countess of Malmesbury, who died in 1877, occupying the
place of the sedilia; and on the north the exquisite chantry of
Margaret, Countess of Salisbury, the last bearer of the royal
name of Plantagenet, whose tragic fate and horrible execution

THE SALISBURY CHANTRY.

is one of the foulest stains on the memory of Henry VIII.
She was the daughter of "false, fleeting, perjured Clarence"
and of the kingmaker's eldest daughter Isabella, and was
mother of the celebrated Reginald Pole who, being ordained
deacon at the age of sixteen, was appointed Dean of Wimborne a year later, and rose in time to the high rank of
Cardinal-Archbishop of Canterbury, and played an important
part in history in the reigns of Henry VIII. and Mary. She
erected this lovely chantry as her last resting-place, wishing to
lie after her troublous life in this quiet spot, but it was not so to
be. Her son, by the publication on the Continent of a violent
attack on Henry VIII., incensed the king to such an extent
that he laid his hands on all the kindred of the Poles he
could find in England ; some were tried and executed, others
attainted without trial, among them the Countess of Salisbury,
who was at the time over seventy years of age. She refused
to lay her head upon the block, and the headsman hacked at
her neck as she stood erect ; her body was not allowed to be
buried in the chantry which she had erected for herself,— so far
did the spite of Henry go,—but she lies among the ambitious
and unfortunate, the aspiring, and unsuccessful of many a sect
and party in the cemetery of St Peter's Chapel in the Tower.
Hers was an ill-starred race. Her grandfather was slain at
Barnet, 1471 ; her father murdered by his brother Edward IV.,
1478 ; her own brother, the Earl of Warwick, imprisoned by
Henry VII., and subsequently beheaded on Tower Hill, 1499 ;
her eldest son, Lord Montagu, was executed for high treason ;
and Margaret herself met a like fate on May 27, 1541.

Her chantry is built of Caen stone, and the decoration is
of Renaissance character. It is conjectured to be the work of
the Florentine sculptor Pietro Torrigiano, who died in the
prison of the Inquisition in Spain in 1522. He was engaged
on Henry VII.'s tomb in Westminster, and other works ordered
by Henry VIII. at Westminster and Windsor, from 1509 till
1517 ; and if this chantry at Christchurch is his design the
date must lie between these two years. Two four-light
windows with battlemented transoms look out on either side ;
to the west of these two doorways lead, one to the presbytery
the other to the north aisle ; on the east wall are three canopied
niches, beneath which an altar stood or was intended to stand ;
the ceiling is richly carved with fan traceries and bosses ; the

latter have been mutilated—by order, it is said, of Henry VIII.
A letter from the King's Commissioner thus describes the work
done :—" In thys churche we founde a chaple and a monumet

INTERIOR OF THE SALISBURY CHANTRY.

curiosly made of cane stone p'pared by the late mother of
Raynolde Pole for herre buriall, which we have causyd to be
defaced and all the Armis and Badgis to be delete." On

the north side are twelve tabernacles. This chapel stands on a richly carved panelled basement, and all the walls are covered with minute carving; but here, as elsewhere, in late work we find the same forms repeated again and again, and we miss that wealth of fancy which gives each boss or capital carved by the earlier workers such a life and individuality. The side of this chapel that faces the north aisle is more elaborate than that facing the choir, and is necessarily more lofty, as its base rests on the floor of the aisle, which is lower than the floor of the presbytery. On the west face is one of several memorial tablets to members of the Rose family, who are buried in this aisle.

In the north choir aisle, at the western end, may be seen a kind of small museum of fragments from various parts of the church, collected at the time of the restoration, among them some bosses from the vaulting of the south transept, destroyed about a hundred years ago, and an octagonal Norman font. The vaulting of this and the corresponding aisle on the south side is of the same character as that of the choir, but is somewhat plainer, and is not decorated with crosses or pendants. On the south side of this aisle is a late Perpendicular chantry, the origin of which is not known; on its flat ceiling are painted two large roses, one white, one red; it contains two brackets for cruets; over the entrance to it is placed an oval memorial tablet to one John Cook, who died in 1787. Eastward of this is the Salisbury chapel already described. A chantry is formed at the eastern end of the aisle by the western end of the north wall of the Lady Chapel. It contains an altar tomb with the recumbent figures of Sir John Chidioke, a Dorset knight slain in 1449 in the Wars of the Roses, and his wife. This monument has occupied its present position only from 1791,—it previously stood in the north transept.

The east end of the south choir aisle is occupied by the chantry chapel of John Draper II., the last of the priors and titular bishop of Neapolis in Palestine, near the ancient Shechem in Samaria; it is dated 1529, and is formed by a screen of Caen stone stretching across the aisle. There is a central doorway with a depressed arch at the top, and canopied niches over it, and on either side are two transomed four-light unglazed windows under arches of the same characters as that over the doorway; along the top of the screen runs a battlemented

THE DRAPER CHANTRY.

parapet. Within the chantry, on the south wall, is a very beautiful piscina, the finest in the church. Just outside the screen is a square-headed doorway. Along the south wall of this aisle, as along the north wall of the corresponding north aisle, a stone bench-table runs. On the north side the panelled wall on which the Countess of Malmesbury's altar tomb stands is decorated with carvings of angels; the largest of these holds a shield with a death's-head. Farther to the west, beyond the steps leading down from the choir, is a Perpendicular chantry, known as the Harys chantry; it has open tracery above cusped panels, canopied niches, and a panelled bench table. Robert Harys was rector of Shrowston, and died in 1525; his rebus, a hare under the letter R, may be seen on the panels. On the opposite side of the aisle is the doorway leading into what is known as the sacristy. This is a thirteenth-century addition to the church, and is of irregular shape, as it is wedged in, as it were, between the apsidal chapel on the east side of the transept and the south wall of the choir aisle. In the south wall are triple sedilia with Purbeck shafts and foliated heads; in the north wall is a square opening or squint.

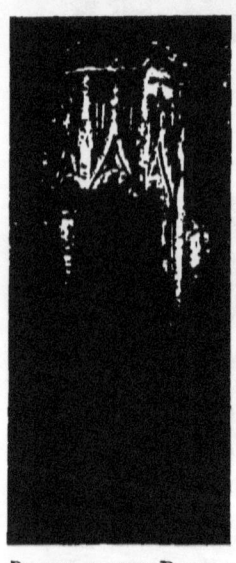

PISCINA IN THE DRAPER CHANTRY.

Behind the reredos is an ambulatory or processional path; from this may be seen, over the archway leading into the south aisle, the end of the "miraculous beam," lengthened, according to the legend, by Christ, when He appeared as a workman and took part in the building of the original church. How this came to be preserved, and how it came to occupy a position amidst the latest work in the church, is not recorded. The Lady Chapel is very beautiful Perpendicular work; it had its own altar and reredos under the east window. The reredos is much mutilated, but besides the part that is still attached to the wall, there are many loose fragments now set up on the altar. This is a

THE SACRISTY.

slab of Purbeck stone, 11 ft. in length and 3 ft. 10 ins
in breadth.   On the north and south sides of the altar
are the tombs of Thomas, Lord West, and Lady Alice West,
his mother.   These tombs are of Purbeck marble and of a
form by no means uncommon in the churches of Wessex.
The ten shafts supporting the canopy of the tomb on the

north still remain ; from
the other tomb such
shafts as it had have
disappeared.   Thomas,
Lord West, died in
1406, his mother in
1395 : these dates fix
within reasonable limits
the date of the building
of the Lady Chapel.
Thomas West, in his
will, directs that his
body should be buried
in the " *New* Chapel
of Our Lady in the
Mynster of Christ-
church."   It is note-
worthy to remark that
the original arcading is
cut away to make room
for this monument, so
that the chapel had
been finished before
he died.   Both Sir
Thomas West and his
mother were benefac-

THE MIRACULOUS BEAM.

tors to the church.
Besides other bequests
of money towards the building fund and for perpetual
masses, each of them gave about £18 for the singing
of 4500 masses within six months of the day of their
deaths.   On the south side of the chapel is the original
doorway leading into the canons' burial-ground ; a corresponding door is to be seen on the north side.   The splays of
the arches of the windows are elaborately ornamented with

THE TOMB OF THOMAS, LORD WEST.

panelling.   The arcading under the window, a series of ogee
arches, is worthy of notice.   The tattered colours of the

THE LADY CHAPEL.

"Loyal Christchurch Volunteers," one of the earliest regi-
ments of volunteers, which was enrolled in 1793, hang at the
entrance to the Lady Chapel.   The vaulting is of the same

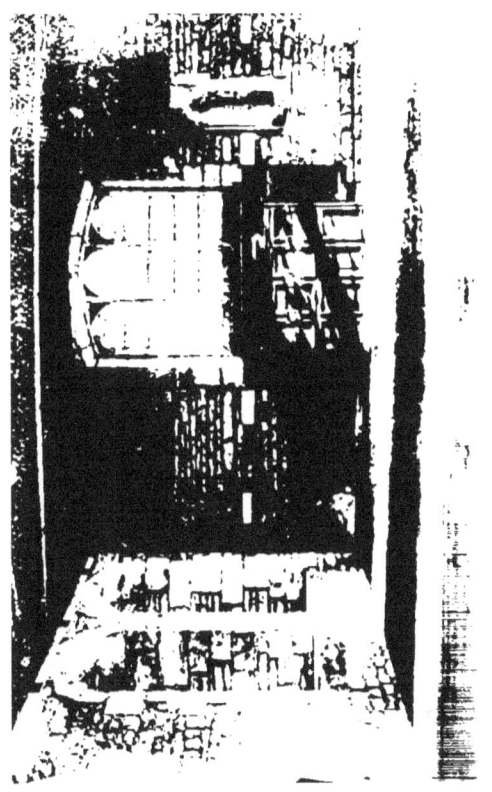

character as that of the choir, with curious pendants in the form of church lanterns.

St Michael's Loft is reached by long flights of steps running up the turrets described in the last chapter. It is a plain, low room with a low-pitched tie-beam roof of oak. It was once a chapel, as the piscina in the east wall clearly shows. The site of the altar is now occupied by a disused desk of the character familiar to us in our own school days some half-a-century ago; it is a sort of pew with doors, within which the master sat enthroned and ramparted. This room was used as a public grammar school from 1662 till 1828, and subsequently as a private school, which was finally closed in 1869. The boys went to this school and returned from it by the staircase on the north side which has an entrance from the churchyard; the stairs on the south side were used when anyone had occasion to go into the church or to go from it to the room above.

An upper chamber or chapel is an uncommon feature in England. Remains of staircases give rise to the conjecture that there was a similar chapel over the Lady Chapel at Chester, and somewhat similar erections are to be met with on the Continent; but Christchurch Priory is unique in possessing such a perfect specimen. The dedication of the upper storey to St Michael, the conductor of souls to Paradise, is appropriate. Churches built in elevated positions were frequently dedicated to him, and few if any mediæval churches dedicated to this archangel are to be met with on low-lying ground.

Under the western tower stands a modern font. The fragments of a Norman font, with carvings representing various incidents in the life of Christ, may be seen, preserved in the north choir aisle. The fifteenth-century successor has been removed to Bransgore Church, four miles off.

Against the north wall of the tower stands the monument of the poet Shelley, the work of the sculptor Weekes. Needless to say, it is but a cenotaph. The "heart of hearts," "Cor Cordium," and the ashes of the poet cremated on the Tuscan shore, lie far away, hard by the pyramid of Caius Cestius, in the grave where the loving hands of Trelawney laid them in 1823. Here we have an ideal representation of the finding of the drowned body—not a pleasing one, but less ghastly than the reality; and below the inscription which tells his name and the number of his years and the manner of his death, the following stanza from his own "Adonais" may be read : —

> " He hath out-soared the shadow of our night :
> Envy and calumny and hate and pain,
> And that unrest which men miscall delight,
> Can touch him not and torture not again ;
> From the contagion of the world's slow stain
> He is secure, and now can never mourn
> A heart grown cold, a head grown grey in vain,
> Nor, when the spirit's self has ceased to burn
> With sparkless ashes load an unlamented urn."

The choice of Christchurch Priory as the site for this monument was due to the fact that the poet's son, Sir Percy Florence Shelley, who erected it, lived at Boscombe Manor, between Christchurch and Bournemouth.

The tower contains a peal of eight bells. These are all old; the fifth and sixth bells have fourteenth-century inscriptions round their crowns, the others appear to have been cast early in the fifteenth century.

CHAPTER IV

DEANS OF THE SECULAR COLLEGE

1. Ralf Flambard, afterwards Bishop of Durham.
2. Godric, 1099.
3. Gilbert de Dousgunels, 1100.
4. Peter de Oglander.
5. Randulphus.
6. Hilary, afterwards Bishop of Chichester.

PRIORS OF THE AUGUSTINIAN COLLEGE

1. Reginald, 1150.
2. Ralph.
3. Peter, 1195. He built the clerestory and carried out other Early English work.
4. Roger, 1225.
5. Richard.
6. Nicholas de Wareham.
7. Nicholas de Sturminster.
8. John de Abingdon, 1272.
9. William de Netheravon, 1278.
10. Richard Maury, 1286.
11. William Quenton, 1302.
12. Walter Tholveshide, 1317.
13. Edmund de Ramsbury, 1323. During his time Bishop Stratford's Injunctions were issued, 1325. See page 129.
14. Richard de Queteshorne, 1337.
15. Robert de Leyghe, 1340.
16. William Tyrewache, 1345.
17. Henry Eyre, 1357. He became blind in 1367 and was allowed a coadjutor.
18. John Wodenham, 1376.
19. John Borard, 1398. During his time Archbishop Arundel issued Injunctions, 1404. See page 130.

20. Thomas Talbot, 1413.
21. John Wimborne, 1420.
22. William Norton.
23. John Dorchester.
24. John Draper I., 1477. Bishop Langton's Injunctions were issued during his tenure of the priory.
25. William Eyre, 1502. During his time the choir was completed.
26. John Draper II. He surrendered the priory to Henry VIII.'s commissioners, 1539, and was allowed to retain Somerford Grange for life, and received a pension of £133, 6s. 8d. He died in 1552, and was buried in the nave near the entrance to the choir.

VICARS OF CHRISTCHURCH

By the council of Arles 1261, religious orders that held parish churches were bound to supply vicars to officiate. These were appointed by the canons, and were taken from their own body.

The names of many of these are known. The 13th was Robert Harys, whose chantry stands in the south choir aisle; he died in 1325. In the time of the 15th, William Trapnell, the church was granted by Henry VIII. to the parishioners, 32nd year of Henry VIII. In the time of the 17th, Robert Newman, an inventory of the property was made by order of Edward VI.'s commissioner. John Imber, the 21st vicar, was expelled by the Parliament from 1647-1660, but was restored to his preferment in the same year as Charles II. gained the throne. The present vicar is the 32nd.

STRATFORD'S INJUNCTIONS, 1325

1. Every canon save the seneschal and cellarer must attend Matins, High Mass, and the Hours. The seneschal, if present in the priory for two nights together, must attend one Matins, and the cellarer must be present at service on alternate nights at least.

2. Six canons must be enrolled for celebrating Our Lady's Mass; the prior must celebrate on all great feasts at High Mass, and on Saturdays at Our Lady's Mass, and must wear a surplice not a rochet.

I

3. Canons in priests' orders must celebrate daily, those who are not must repeat eleven Psalms with a Litany or Psalter of Our Lady every day.

4. Four confessors must be appointed to hear the confessions of the canons.

5. Latin or French must be the languages spoken.

6. No one save the prior or officers, without special leave, must ride or leave the Priory.

7. Two-thirds of the canons must dine daily in the refectory ; the door must be kept by a secular watchman whose duty it is to remove servants and idle people from the door during dinner; the almoner must prevent any canon carrying his commons to the laundry-people or people of the town.

8. All the canons must sleep in the dormitory, each in his own bed.

9. The infirmary must be visited daily by the prior or sub-prior.

10. Two canons must act as treasurers, and a yearly account must be presented.

11. The common seal must be kept under four locks, and documents sealed in full chapter, not as heretofore during Mass.

12. Canons must not play at chess or draughts, nor keep hounds or arms (save in the custody of the prior), nor have a servant (save when on a journey), nor write nor receive letters without leave. The prior may keep hounds outside the priory buildings.

ARCHBISHOP ARUNDEL'S INJUNCTIONS, 1404

No. 1. Ordered the destruction of an old hall and an adjoining chamber known as the sub-prior's hall after the departure of Sir Thomas West its then occupier, as noblemen were in the habit of occupying it to the great disturbance of the order and the keeping open of gates which ought to be closed.

No. 2. Enjoined the building of a house for the præcentor, and a new chamber for the sick.

No. 3. Ordered the setting apart of a chamber for recreation apart from the infirmary (it may be supposed that the canons during recreation hours were noisy, thereby disturbing the sick).

No. 4. Directed the provision of separate studies for the canons. It would appear that nobles, such as the Montacutes and Wests, put the priory to such great expense by taking up their abode, together with their retainers, in the domestic part of the buildings.

THE NORMAN CASTLE

Very little of the castle erected by Richard de Redvers, who died in 1137, remains; but on an artificial mound at no great distance to the north of the Priory Church stand fragments of the east and west walls of the square Norman keep, about 20 feet high and 10 feet thick. The castle belonged to the De Redvers, Earls of Devon, till they were alienated to the crown in the 9th year of Edward I. (1280), the last earl having died in 1263, though the last female descendant lived till 1293. In 1331, Edward III. granted the castle and land to William de Montacute, Earl of Salisbury; after the execution of John de Montacute in 1400 for the part he took in the plots against the new king, Henry IV., Sir Thomas West, who lies buried in the Lady Chapel, was appointed constable. He died in 1405, then Thomas, Earl of Salisbury, held the castle till 1428. After this it was held by various persons, and we find a constable of the Lordship of Christchurch as late as 1656. The manor held by the De Redvers, and then by the Montacutes, passed through various hands. Among the holders we may notice the Nevilles, hence the connection with the Priory of the ill-fated Margaret, the kingmaker's granddaughter, who was Countess of Salisbury in her own right, the Earl of Clarendon, Sir George Rose, and the present owner, the Earl of Malmesbury, who obtained it in 1862.

In early days the bailiff of the de Redvers regulated all markets, fairs, tolls, and fines, and had the right of preemption and sat as judge in the tenants' court. Edward I. relieved the burgesses of Christchurch from all arbitrary exactions, and established a fixed fee-farm rent instead. The castle was taken for the Parliament by Sir William Waller with 300 men on April 7, 1644.

A little to the north-east of the castle stand the remains of one of the few Norman houses that have come down to the present time. It is thus described in the first volume of

"The Domestic Architecture of the Middle Ages " by Turner and Parker, pp. 38, 39.   This volume was published in 1851. "At Christchurch, in Hampshire, is the ruin of a Norman house, rather late in the style, with good windows of two lights and a round chimney shaft.*   The plan, as before, is a simple oblong; the principal room appears to have been on the first floor.   It is situated on the bank of the river near to the church, and still more close to the mound, which is said to have been the keep of the castle; being between that and the river, it could not well have been placed in a situation of greater security.   Whether it formed part of another series of buildings or not, it was a perfect house in itself, and its character is strictly domestic.   It is about seventy feet long, and twenty-four broad, its walls, like those of the keep, being exceedingly thick.   On the ground floor are a number of loop-holes : the ascent to the upper storey was by a stone staircase, part of which remains ; the ground floor was divided by a wall, but the upper storey seems to have been a long room, lighted by three double windows on each side ; near the centre of the east wall, next the river, is a large fireplace, to which the round chimney before mentioned belongs.   At the north end, there appears to have been a large and hand-some window of which part of the arch and shafts remain, and there is a small circular window in the south gable. From what remains of the ornamental part of this building, it appears to have been elegantly finished and cased with squared stones, most of which are, however, now taken away. There is a small projecting tower, calculated for a flank, under which the water runs ; it has loopholes both on the north and east fronts, these walls are extremely thick.   By the ruins of several walls, there were some ancient buildings at right angles to this hall, stretching away towards the keep.   This was probably part of the residence of Baldwin de Redvers, Earl of Devon, to whom the manor of Christchurch belonged about the middle of the twelfth century."†

This building is much overgrown with ivy, which by a comparison of the illustration given in the work just quoted with its present condition, as represented in the photograph here reproduced, has increased considerably during the last

---

* Since rebuilt.
† Grove's " Antiquities," vol. ii. p. 178.

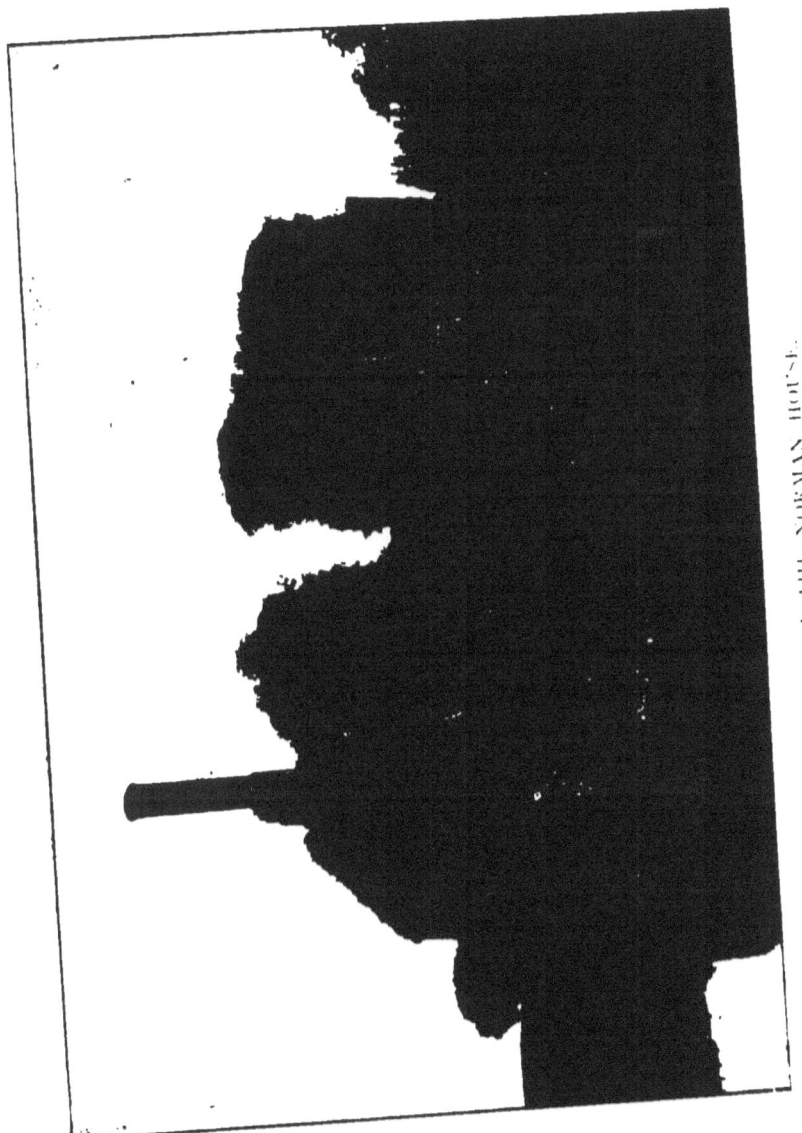

REMAINS OF THE NORMAN HOUSE.

fifty years. It is due to the memory of the Rev. William Jackson, who was vicar of Christchurch from 1778 to 1802, that it should be recorded that he saved this valuable relic of Norman domestic architecture from destruction. He was evidently imbued with a spirit of love for antiquity by no means common a hundred years ago, and far too rare even at the present day.

DIMENSIONS OF CHRISTCHURCH PRIORY

Extreme length . . .	311 feet.
Length of Nave . . .	118 ,, 9 inches.
Width of Nave . . .	58 ,, 5 ,,
Height of Nave . . .	58 ,,
Length of Transept . . .	101 ,, 2 ,,
Width of Transept . . .	24 ,, 4 ,,
Length of Choir . . .	70 ,,
Width of Choir with Aisles . .	60 ,, 6 ,,
Height of Choir . . .	63 ,,
Length of side of Tower, E. to W. .	27 ,, 9 ,,
,, ,, ,, N. to S. .	22 ,, 4 ,,
Height of Tower . . .	120 ,,
Length of Lady Chapel . .	36 ,, 4 ,,
Width of Lady Chapel . .	21 ,, 1 ,,
Length of St Michael's Loft .	58 ,, 3 ,,
Width of St Michael's Loft . .	19 ,, 7 ,,
AREA	18,300 sq. feet.

PLANS

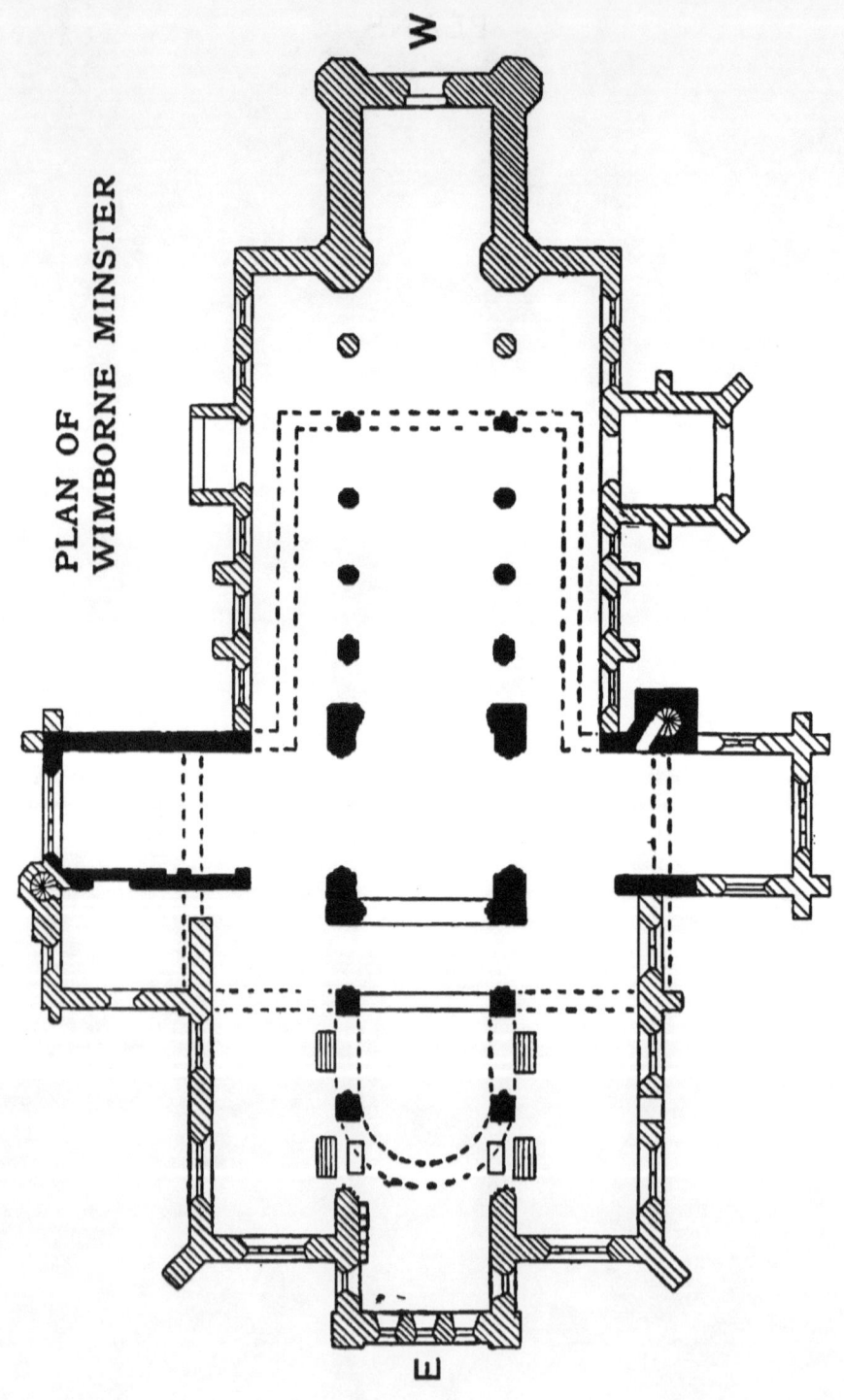

PLAN OF WIMBORNE MINSTER

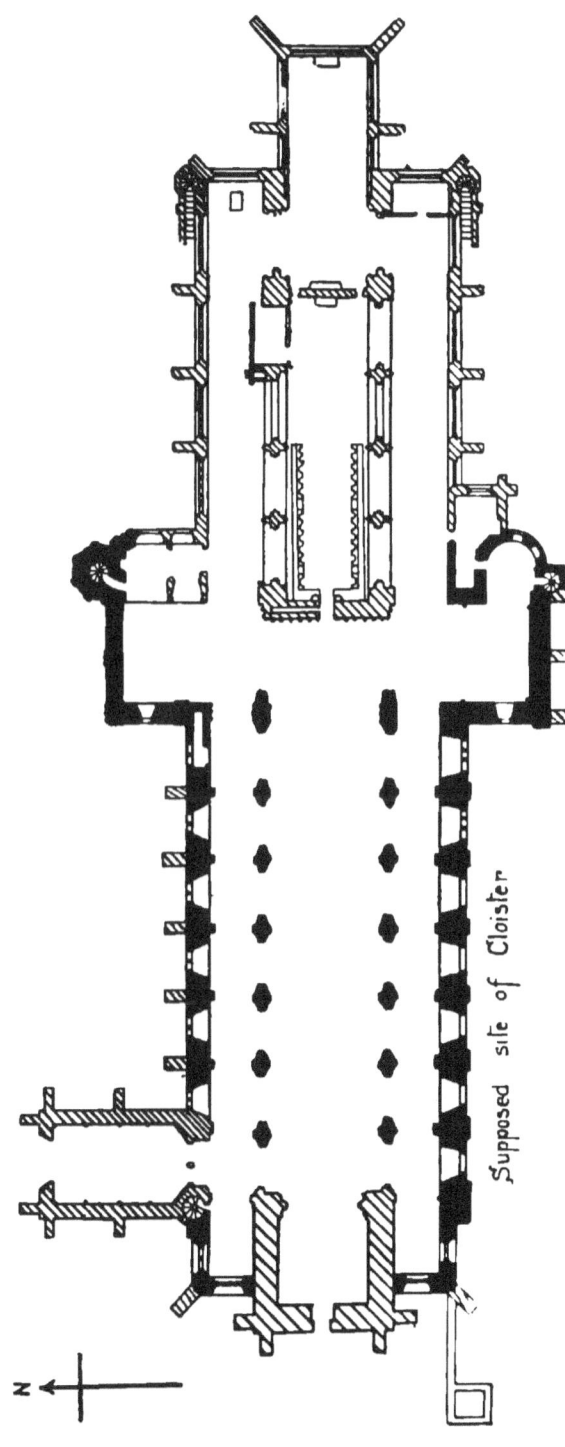

Supposed site of Cloister

PLAN OF CHRISTCHURCH PRIORY

W. H. WHITE AND CO. LIMITED
RIVERSIDE PRESS, EDINBURGH